THE ART DOODLE BOOK

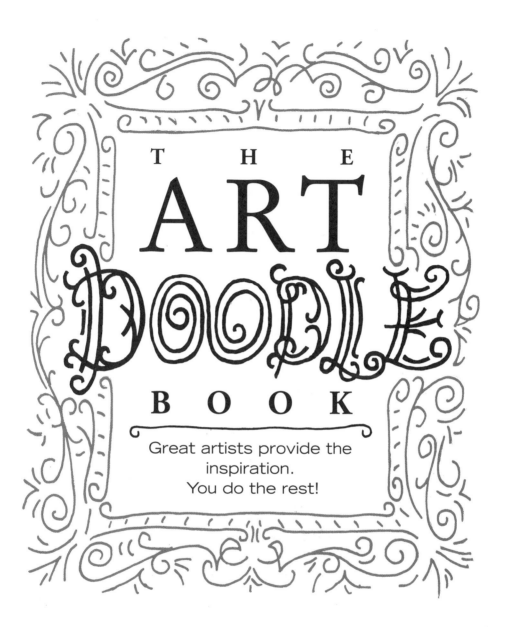

THE ART DOODLE BOOK

Great artists provide the
inspiration.
You do the rest!

ABRAMS IMAGE, NEW YORK

Artists' biographies: Liz Scoggins
Picture research: Judith Palmer
Cover redesign: Galen Smith
Interior redesign: Alissa Faden

Library of Congress Cataloging-in-Publication Data

The art doodle book.
      p. cm.
 ISBN 978-0-8109-7087-8
 1. Doodles. 2. Artists' preparatory studies.

 NC915.D6A745 2008
 741.2—dc22
                            2007041799

First published in 2007 by Buster Books, an imprint of Michael O'Mara Books Limited,
9 Lion Yard, Tremadoc Road, London SW4 7NQ

Published in the United States in 2008 by Abrams Image, an imprint of Harry N. Abrams, Inc.

Printed and bound in China

10 9 8 7 6 5 4 3 2 1

HNA ▐▐▐▐▐
harry n. abrams, inc.
a subsidiary of La Martinière Groupe
Harry N. Abrams, Inc.
115 West 18th Street
New York, NY 10011
www.hnabooks.com

Why You'll Love The Art Doodle Book

Do you enjoy doodling? Have you ever wished you could be an artist? Either way, *The Art Doodle Book* offers all the inspiration you'll need. Simply complete the pictures inside.

Ideal for all ages, from children to adults, and all levels of ability, from doodlers to budding artists. Uncover your creativity and, along the way, discover the work and techniques of some of the world's great artists.

With over eighty pictures for you to create and complete, *The Art Doodle Book* contains starting points for your drawings and ideas, each inspired by a particular artist.

Choose how to complete your masterpieces, whether by imitating an artist's style or by doodling and drawing in a style of your own.

Look out for the different techniques used: the type of marks an artist makes, the thickness of line, or the amount of shading or detail. Use a variety of materials to draw with, such as pencils, a biro, charcoal, or a felt-tipped pen. Add color if you wish.

On some pages you'll find complete original drawings and paintings to inspire you. Other pages contain only elements of a masterpiece and it is up to you to complete it, whether by guessing what the artist was intending or by drawing something entirely new of your own.

In no time at all, by interacting with the work of great artists, you'll uncover techniques, skills, and a creativity that you never knew you had.

Make your own masterpieces, inspired by these great artists:

PICASSO	LÉGER
MATISSE	HOKUSAI
WARHOL	HARING
TOULOUSE-LAUTREC	MARC
KANDINSKY	DEGAS
KLIMT	CAULFIELD
KLEE	BOSCH
CÉZANNE	CHAGALL
VAN GOGH	MORRIS
MIRÓ	REMBRANDT
SCHIELE	HIROSHIGE
MONET	GRIS
MODIGLIANI	DA VINCI

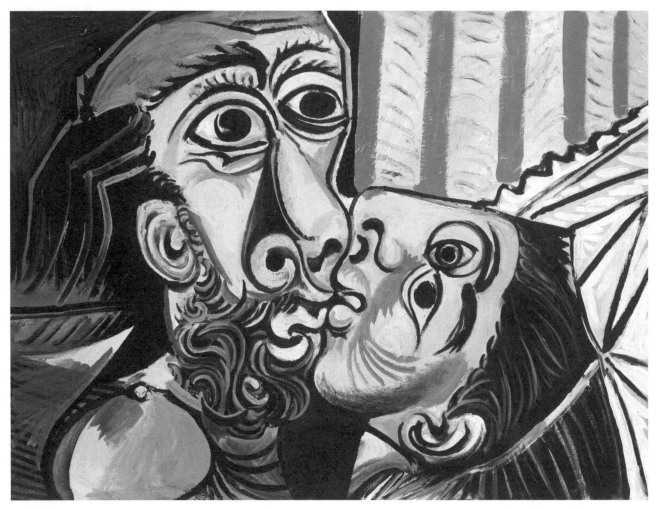

The Kiss, 1969

Picasso
(1881–1973)

The Spanish artist Pablo Picasso discovered the work of van Gogh, Toulouse-Lautrec, and, most importantly, Paul Cézanne when he moved to Paris as a young man. He became friends with the painter Georges Braque, and together the two artists, inspired by Cézanne's paintings, developed Cubism. They left behind traditional techniques to experiment with different viewpoints, opening subjects up so that they could be seen from all angles at once, against the conventions of traditional painting with its single point of perspective. In Spain, Picasso had begun by using simple, natural colors, but once he arrived in France and discovered Cézanne, he went through phases in which he painted in one predominant color, such as blue or pink, although he usually returned to his old Spanish palette. He was also interested in ancient African art, depicting people in the style of the African masks he admired. During his life, Picasso created thousands of paintings, sculptures, and ceramics, and has been an enormous influence on generations of artists.

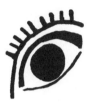

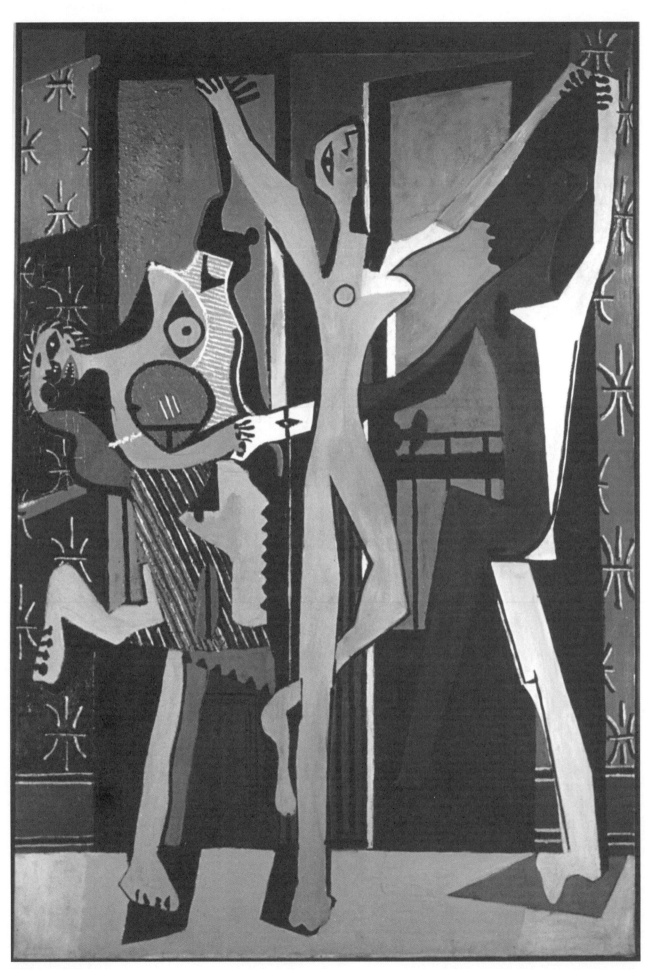

The Three Dancers, 1925

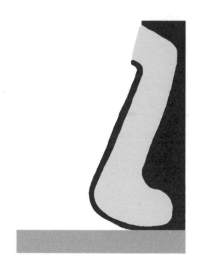

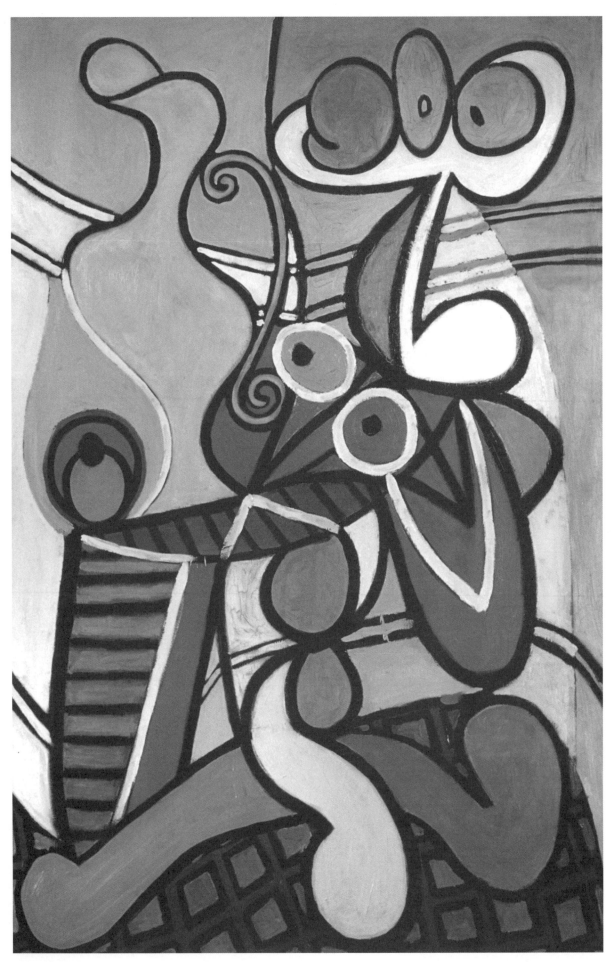

Large Still Life on a Pedestal Table, 1931

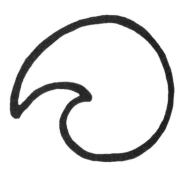

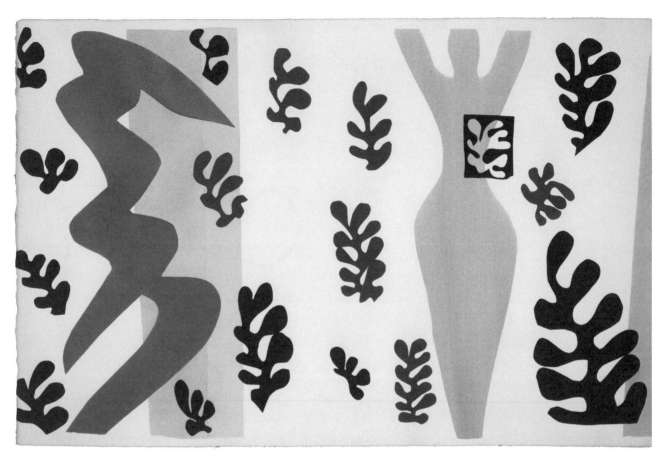

The Knife Thrower, Plate XV from *Jazz*, 1947

Matisse
(1869–1954)

Henri Matisse, the French painter and sculptor, was a leading member of the Fauvists, a group of artists whose name means "wild beasts." In his early paintings, he experimented with Impressionism, and also Pointillism—building up a picture with dots of paint of contrasting colors. Since this was very time-consuming and controlled, Matisse decided to move away from Pointillism. However, he did continue to use a similar approach to color, though on a much larger scale. By simplifying his paintings using a more sparing style, he was able to concentrate on shape and color rather than fussy detail. Reds and greens, oranges and blues jostled each other in large, floating shapes. He liked to use vivid colors side by side to make bright, startling effects with big, sweeping strokes of his brush. As he aged and ill health affected his ability to stand and paint for long periods, Matisse created artworks by a new method, using paper cutouts. He would color paper with paint, cut shapes from the paper, and arrange them to make pictures.

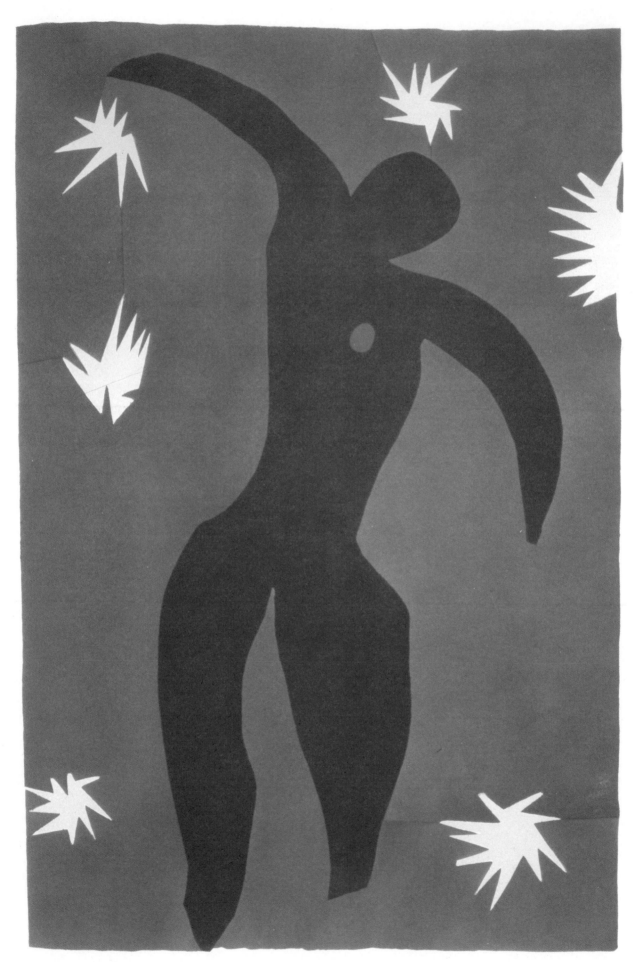

Icarus, Plate VIII from *Jazz*, 1947

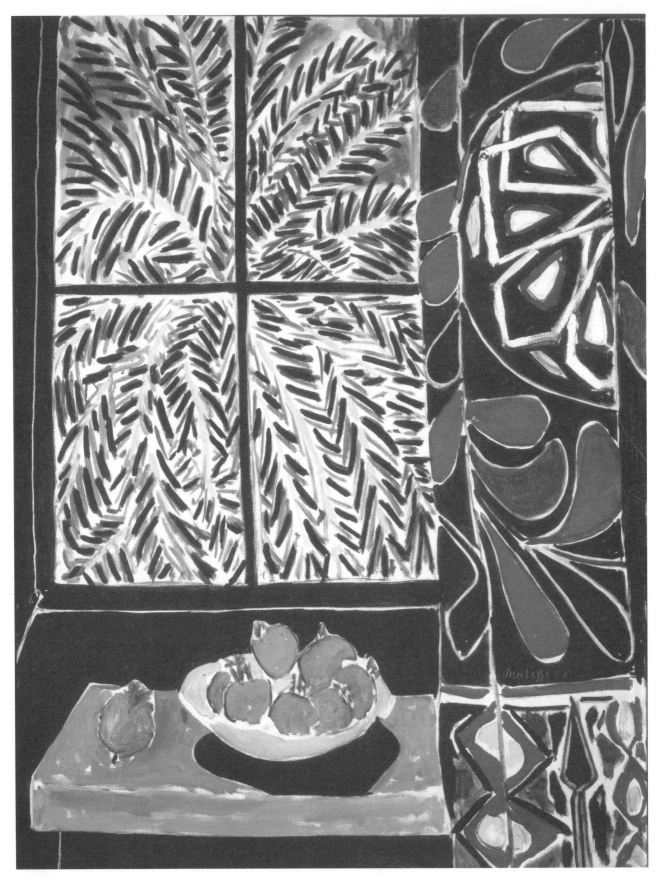

Interior with an Egyptian Curtain, 1948

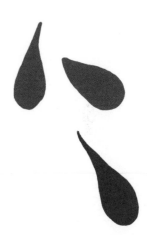

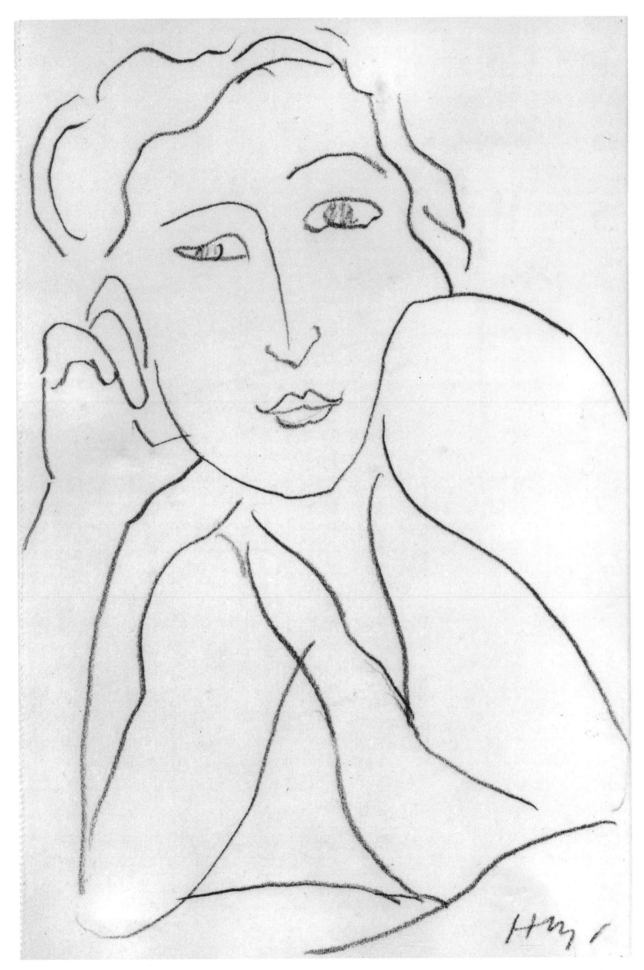

Bust of a Woman with Her Head Resting on Her Hand, 1935

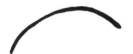

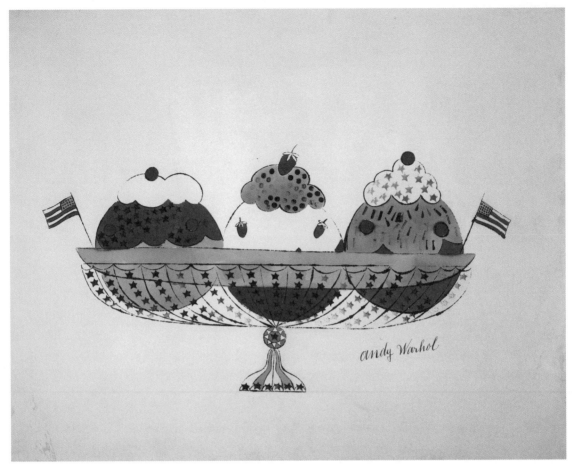

Ice Cream Dessert, c.1959

Warhol

(1928–87)

Pop artist, filmmaker, and cultural icon, Andy Warhol was a talented artist even as a child. He moved to New York City and made his name in advertising and magazine illustration before opening his own studio. His early drawings are very delicate, while his experience in advertising gave him a style that was part graphic design, part painting. In the 1960s he became a leader of the Pop Art movement, and besides making illustrations for ads, he also painted realistic pictures of popular products such as soup and cola cans, thus turning something ordinary and everyday into a work of art. These were a huge success and Warhol started to make them using a silkscreen printing process so that they could be reproduced and more people could own one. His subject matter grew to include celebrities and modern icons, and his portraits of famous people such as Marilyn Monroe, Elizabeth Taylor, and Chairman Mao have been imitated ever since.

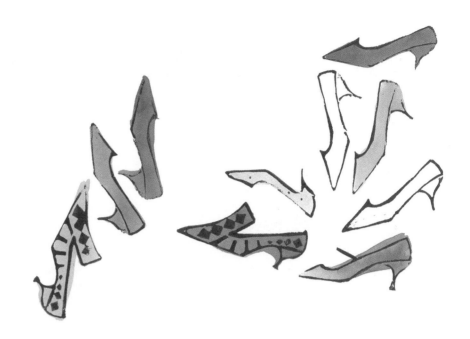

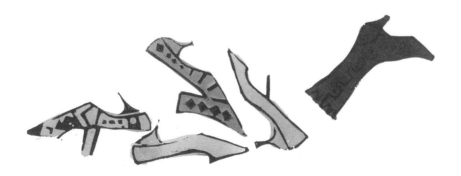

Untitled (Stamped Shoes), c.1959 [detail] © Licensed by the Andy Warhol Foundation for the
Visual Arts, Inc./ARS, New York and DACS, London 2007

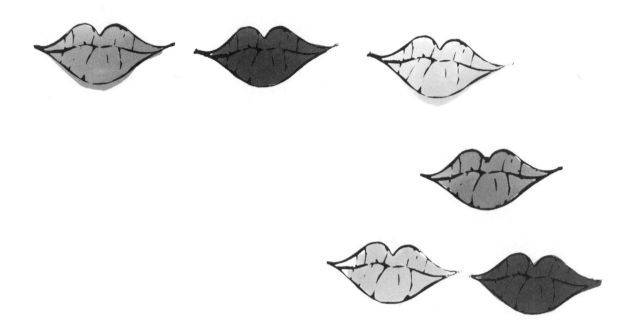

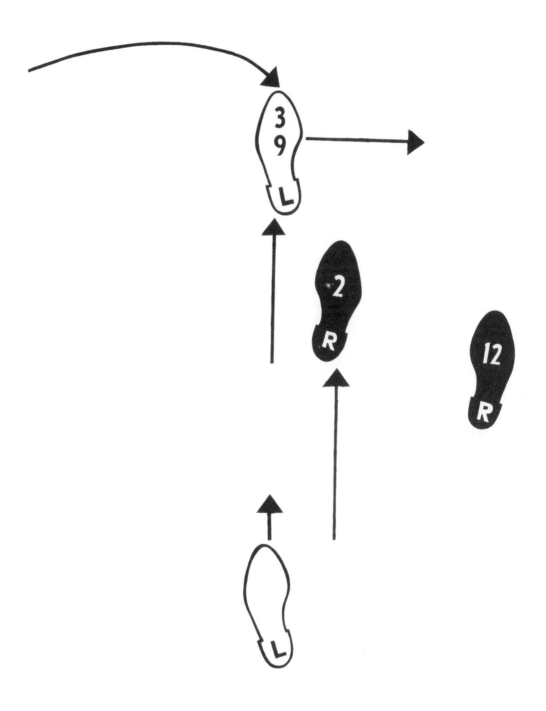

Dance Diagram (Tango), 1962 [detail] © Licensed by the Andy Warhol Foundation
for the Visual Arts, Inc./ARS, New York and DACS, London 2007

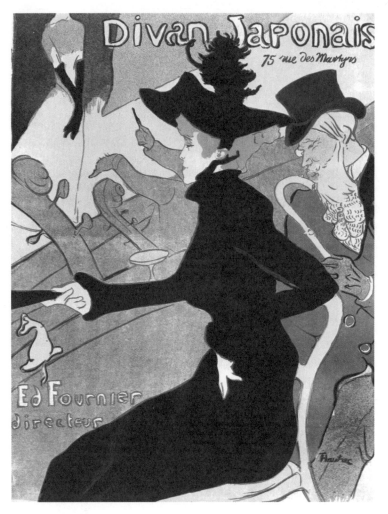

Divan Japonais, 1893

Toulouse-Lautrec
(1864–1901)

Henri-Marie-Raymond de Toulouse-Lautrec-Monfa was born into the French aristocracy, though chose to lead a more bohemian lifestyle in nineteenth-century Paris. His paintings of Parisian life depict subjects ranging from circuses and cafés to the bars and cabarets where he spent his spare time. He developed a style that enabled him to capture the wild and exciting atmosphere of the times, using free-flowing, expressive lines full of movement and energy. Rather than paint people in correct and perfect proportion, Toulouse-Lautrec stylized his figures using solid blocks of color, silhouettes, and flamboyant shapes, lending them a more decorative than realistic appearance. He furthered his style using lithography, a method of printmaking, and at the height of his fame he was creating some of the most iconic poster designs of the Art Nouveau period, which still inspire designers today.

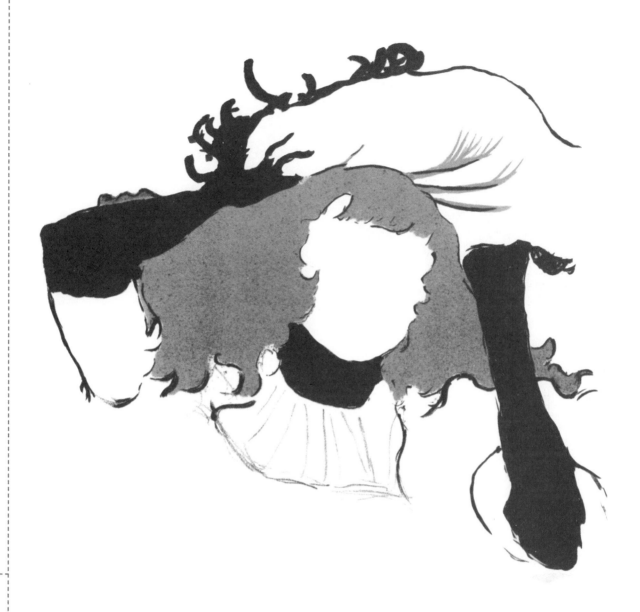

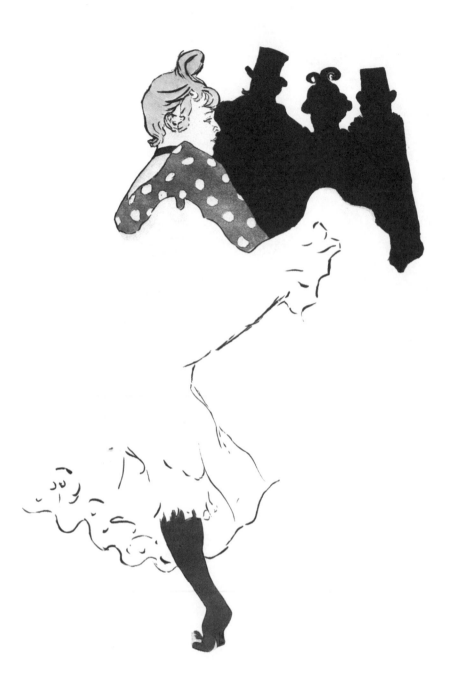

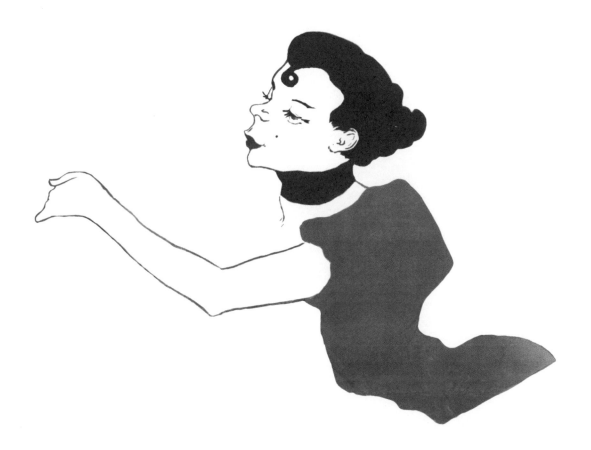

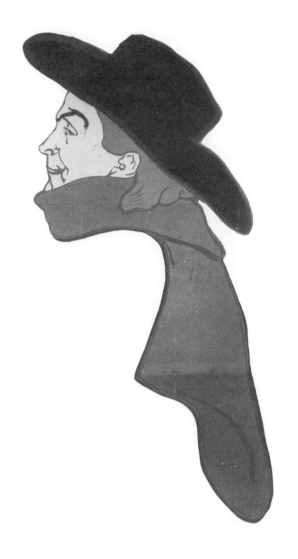

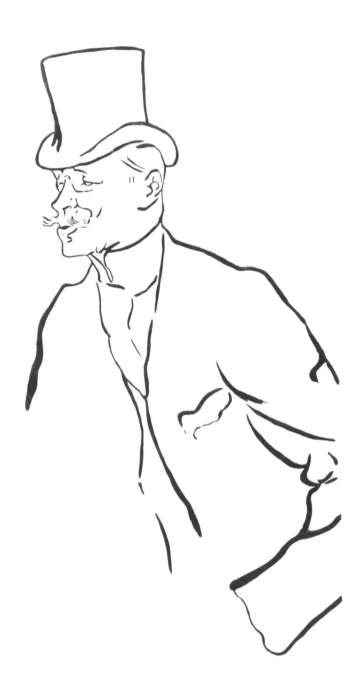

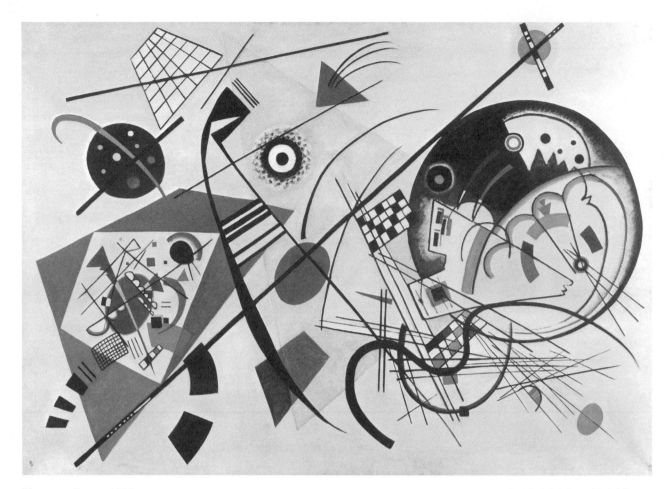

Transverse Line, c.1923

Kandinsky

(1865–1944)

Born in Russia, Wassily Kandinsky did not start painting professionally until he was nearly thirty. His early paintings are quite realistic in their style, but as he developed as an artist his work gradually became more abstract. A founder of the Expressionist Blue Rider group, Kandinsky tried to avoid painting from life, and treated abstract colors and shapes as the important elements in his paintings. He always loved music as well as art, and his choices of colors and shapes are often deliberate visual expressions of music or feelings associated with hearing music. He felt he could hear the sound of a different musical instrument in each color, causing "vibrations in the soul." Kandinsky also developed ideas about the meaning of the lines he painted, as well as the colors. The direction and size of a brushstroke could stand for an emotion or an idea. Because each line and shape meant something to Kandinsky, his images are full of symbols denoting feelings and sensations.

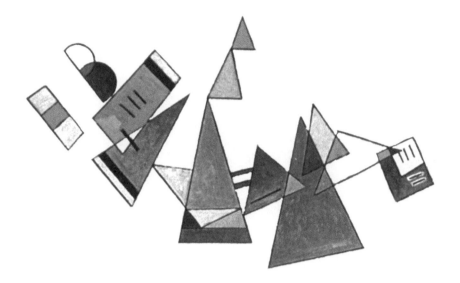

Improvisation, c.1929 [detail] © ADAGP, Paris/DACS 2007

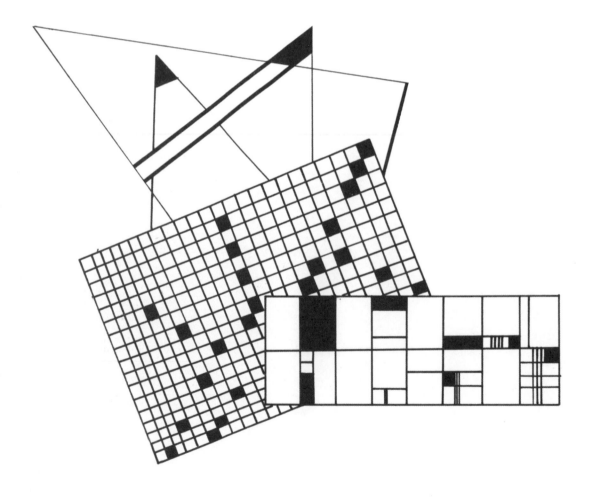

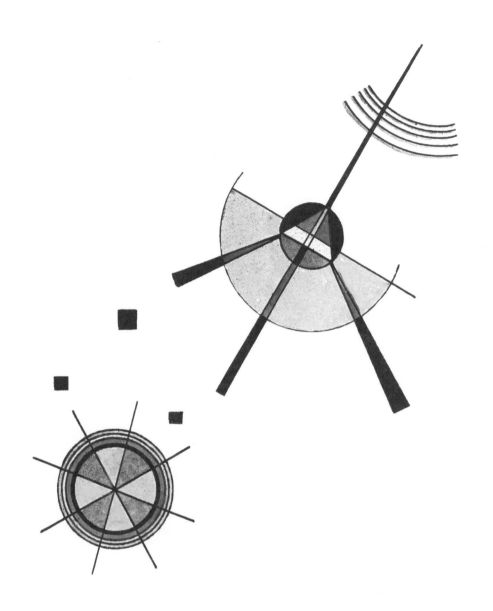

Clear Connection, 1925 [detail] © ADAGP, Paris/DACS 2007

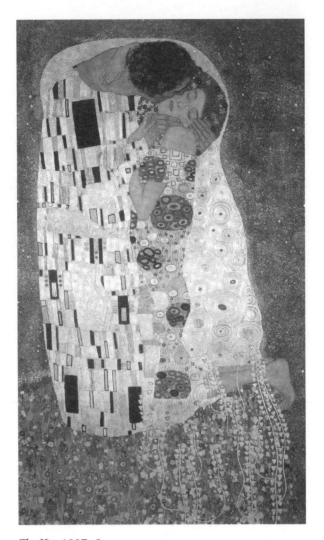

The Kiss, 1907–8

Klimt
(1862–1918)

Gustav Klimt was an Austrian painter who trained as an architectural decorator, receiving commissions to paint murals for Vienna's public buildings. He led the Vienna Secessionist movement, breaking free from the traditional Viennese schools of art. The Secessionists in Austria worked in a similar style to the members of the Art Nouveau movement in France and were interested in creating decorative works. Klimt's themes embraced symbolic interpretations of love, sensuality, and death.

This sometimes made his work too controversial for public display. His figures were painted realistically but in abstract settings, including mosaic-like patterns inspired by ancient art from Greece, Byzantium, and Egypt. It is possible to pick out symbols such as hieroglyphs, delicately mixed with swirling ancient designs. The effect is highly decorative, especially when combined with layers of gold leaf, which Klimt would use frequently.

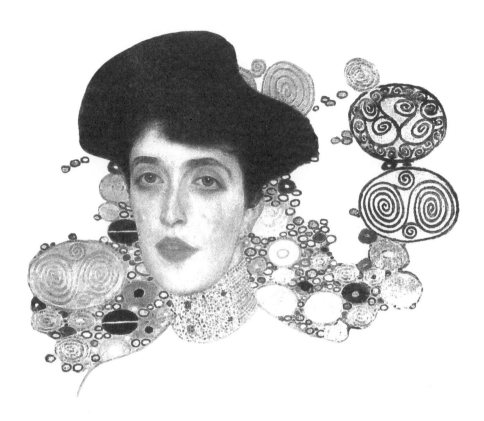

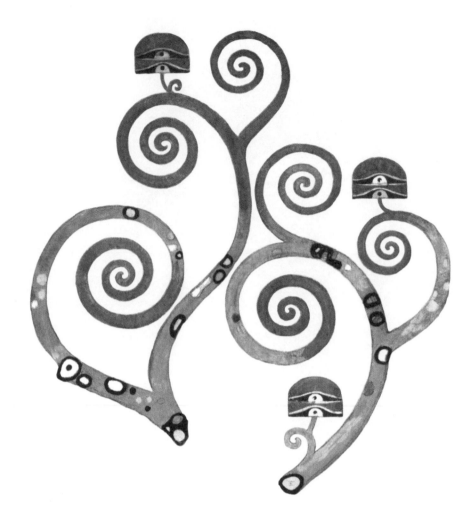

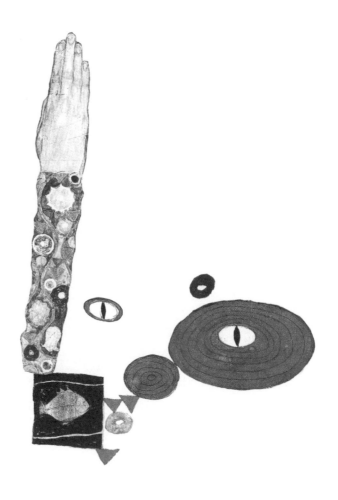

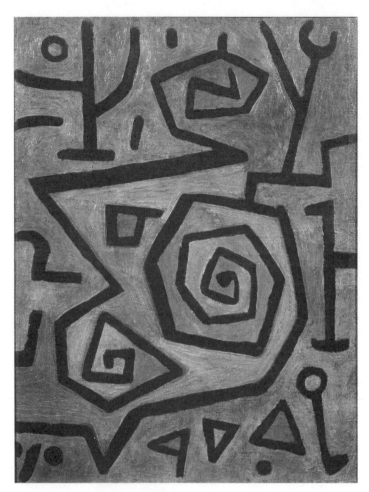

Heroic Roses, 1938 © DACS 2007

Klee
(1879–1940)

Paul Klee grew up in Switzerland, but left for art school in Germany when he was a teenager. Although never really part of any particular art movement, he was influenced by many styles, from Impressionism to Cubism, and was involved with the Expressionist Blue Rider group of artists before the first World War. Klee loved traveling and, after a visit to Tunisia, started to paint with warmer colors, offering bold contrasts between light and dark. He also liked to paint using shapes and letters as symbols, and found inspiration in modern graphic design. Klee was open to widely different ideas from many sources, rather than just from other artists. He admired children's artwork and believed that such paintings were important because children had not been influenced by any strict artistic training. To Klee, this meant that their ideas and imagination were less restricted than his own, leading him to try to replicate a childlike style in his own work.

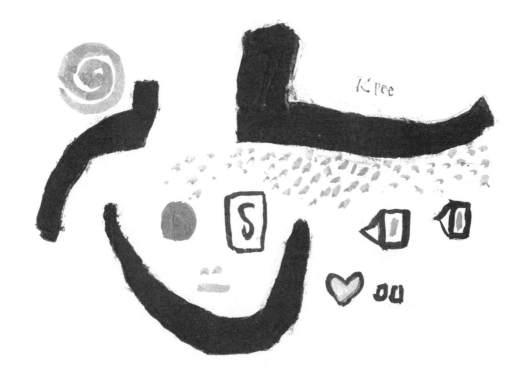

A Children's Game, 1939 [detail] © DACS 2007

KLEE

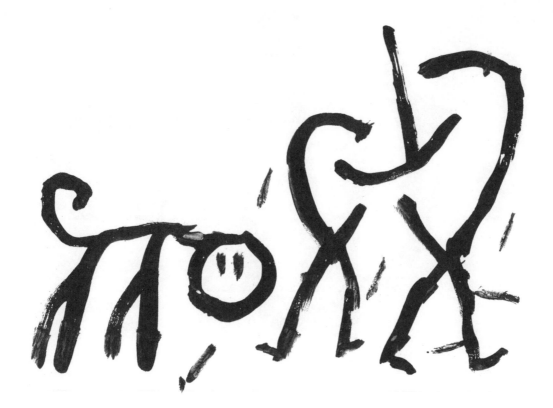

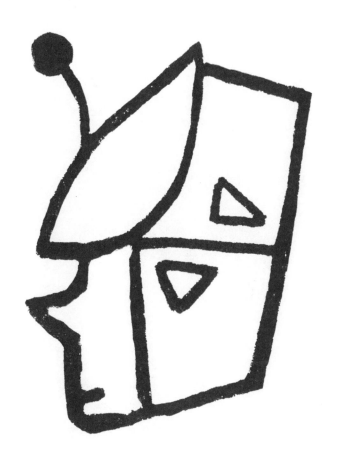

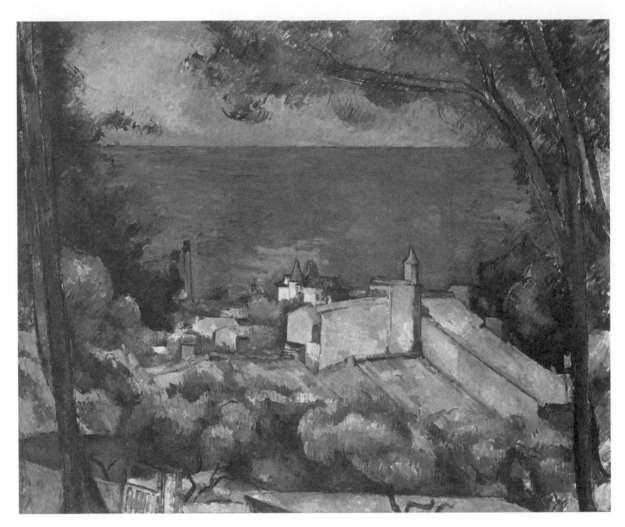

The Sea at L'Estaque, 1886–90

Cézanne
(1839–1906)

The French Post-Impressionist Paul Cézanne developed a style of painting that became hugely influential among other artists. It was Cézanne's theory that all subjects taken from nature could be simplified and shaped in the form of a cylinder, sphere, or cone. He employed clean, bold brushstrokes that were intended to be visible, and built perspective through the use of color alone. He applied the same principles when painting people as he used when creating a landscape, and was generally more interested in the overall effect of the picture than in capturing any likeness of his subject. His idea of reducing aspects of nature to geometric shapes was unique at the time and helped to inspire the artists who would later establish the Cubist movement, including Picasso, who declared Cézanne to be "the father of us all."

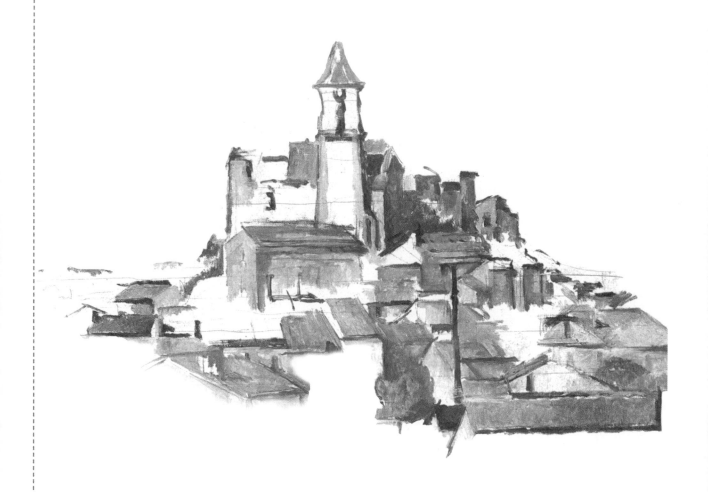

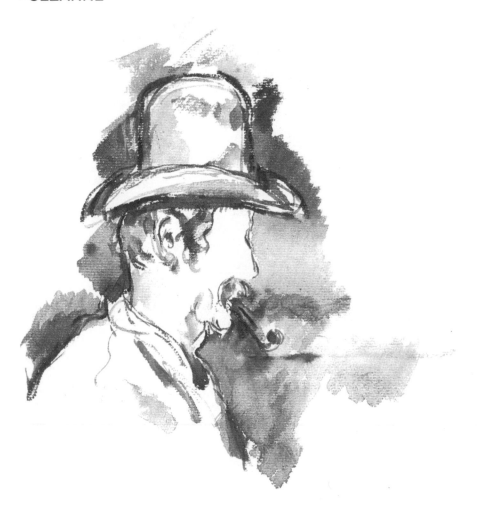

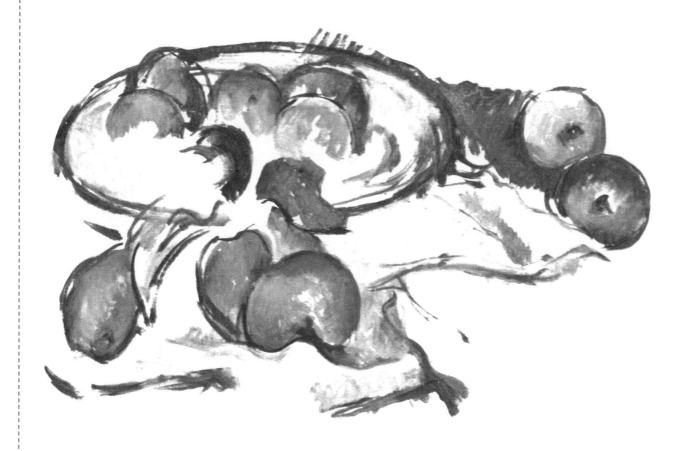

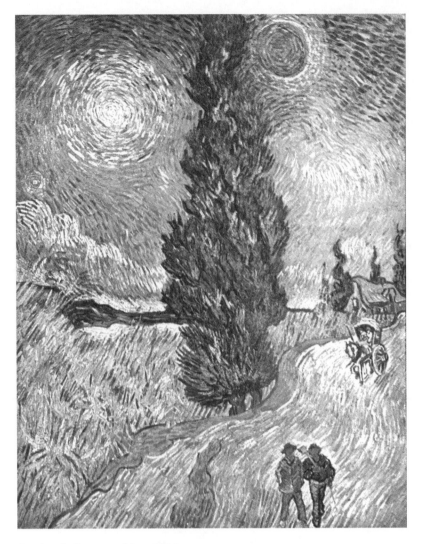

Road with Cypress and Star, 1890

van Gogh
(1853–90)

Vincent van Gogh was a Dutch Post-Impressionist painter who worked as a teacher and an evangelist before devoting his life to art. On moving to Paris to live with his brother, van Gogh took inspiration from the Impressionist movement and developed his signature style, using broken brushstrokes with swirling, vivid, contrasting colors. His painting technique was spontaneous and emotional, conveying moods and atmospheres in movement and texture. On occasion he would even paint straight from the tube, squeezing paint expressively and directly onto the canvas in order to capture the mood of a scene as quickly as possible. His critics, who often remarked that he should paint more slowly, showed little understanding for his methods, and in his lifetime he only ever sold one painting. Today his works command the highest prices.

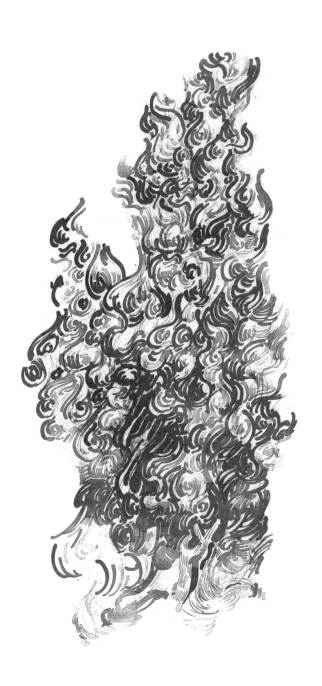

VAN GOGH

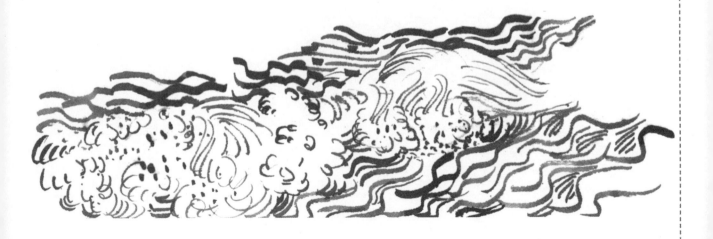

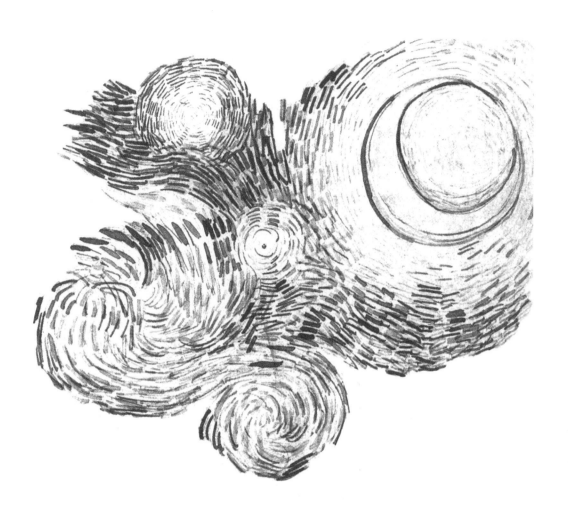

VAN GOGH

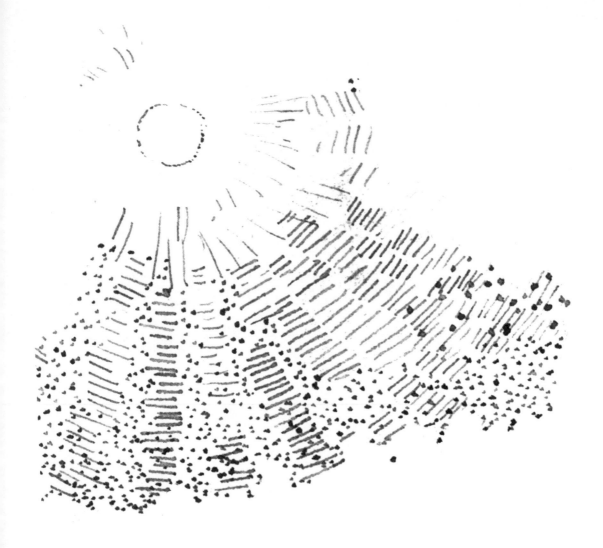

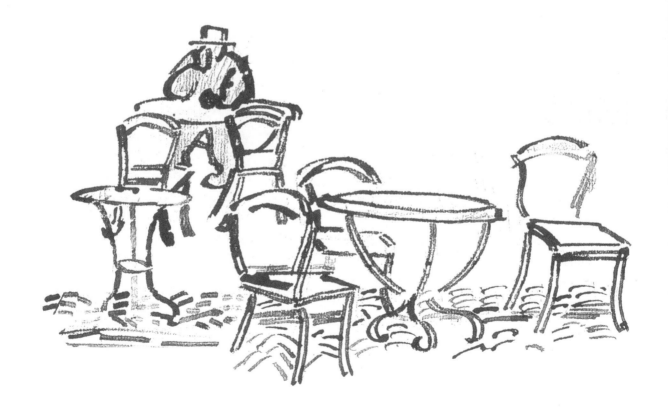

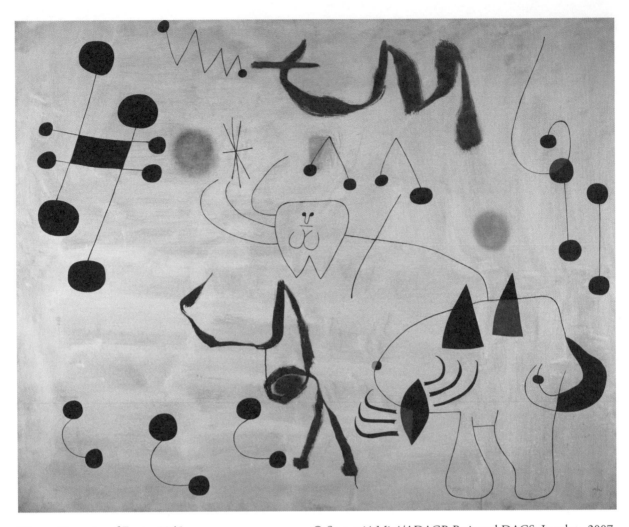

Woman Dreaming of Escape, 1945

© Successió Miró/ADAGP, Paris and DACS, London, 2007

Miró
(1893–1983)

Joan Miró was a Spanish artist, often described as a Surrealist. In fact, he preferred not to be associated with any movement so that he could avoid following other people's ideas about the rules of art, leaving him free to experiment with his own work. He was particularly interested in the art and culture of his native Spain, and especially the work of the architect Antonio Gaudí, who designed colorfully flamboyant buildings and parks in Barcelona. He was also inspired by early primitive art from the region of Catalonia. Miró's paintings seem to imitate these styles in strange, dreamlike scenes of brightly colored, floating forms. He painted very delicately, making round organic shapes surrounded by fine lines and seemingly cartoonlike faces. In some ways his work can look like doodling on a grand scale, but his style was unlike that of any other artist at the time.

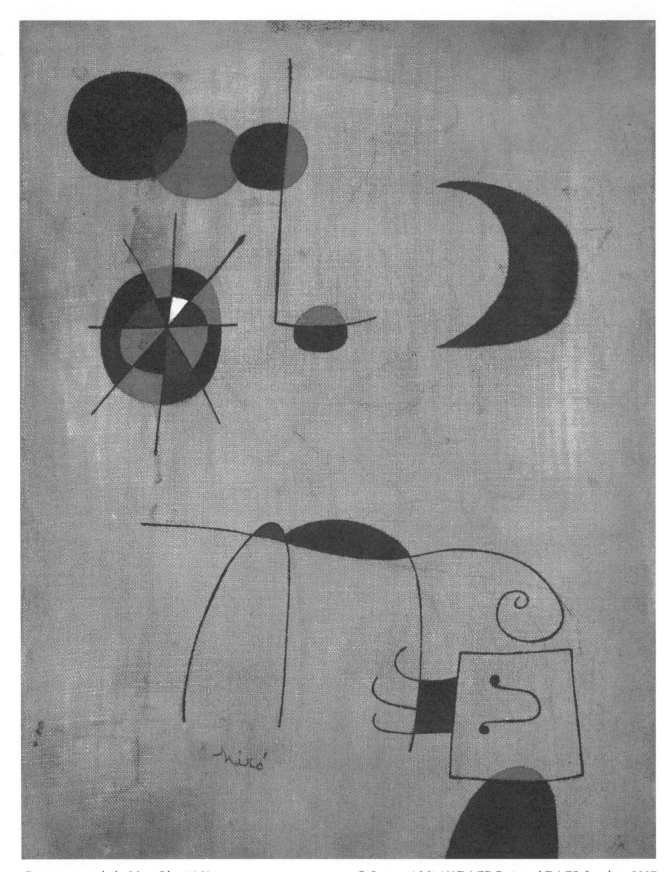

Composition with the Moon Blue, 1949

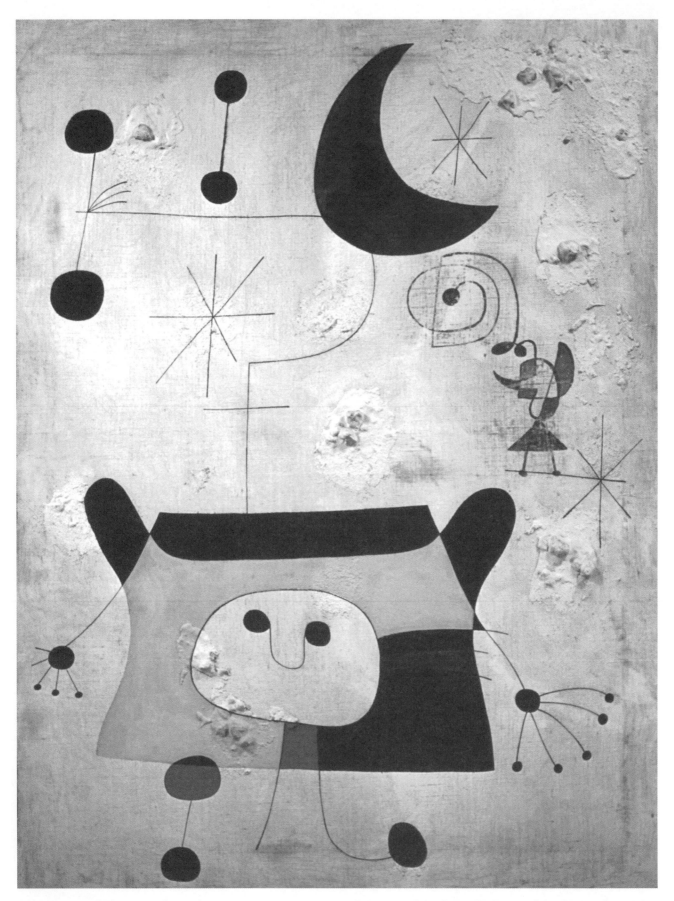

Large Figure and Blue Moon, date unknown

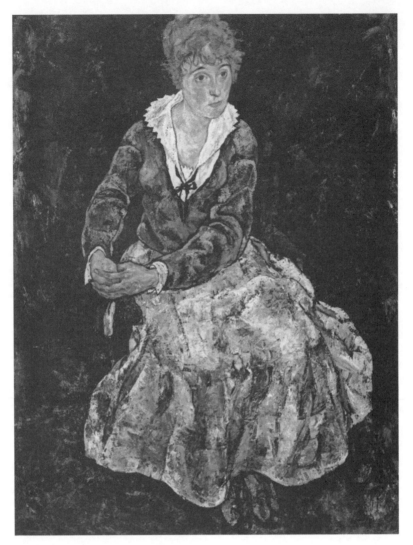

Portrait of the Artist's Wife, Seated, 1918

Schiele
(1890–1918)

Egon Schiele, an Austrian Expressionist painter, was strongly influenced by the German equivalent of the Art Nouveau movement, Jugendstil, but instead of employing such highly decorative techniques, he adopted a much more expressive painting style. An awkward-looking man with strange, ungainly gestures, Schiele's unusual physical appearance is often mirrored by the characters in his pictures. His figures have exaggerated postures and yet are painted with powerfully expressive lines, giving them an angular elegance. Schiele was economical with his brushwork, similar in style to Chinese brush painting, using spare but precise strokes to illustrate the figure. He was often criticized for his choice of subject matter, and at one point in his career was imprisoned for exhibiting paintings of nudes.

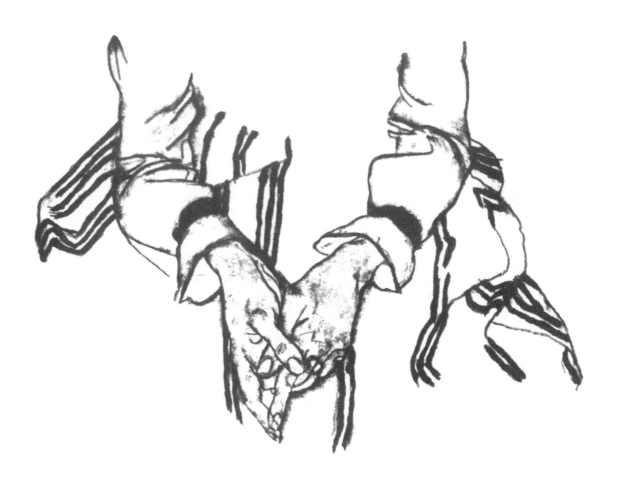

SCHIELE

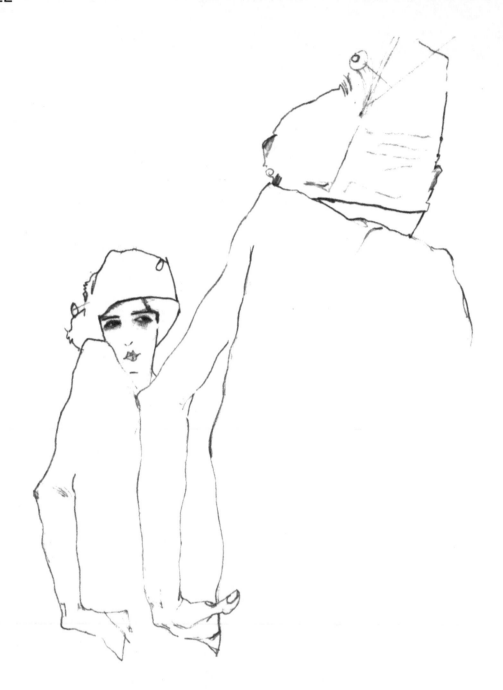

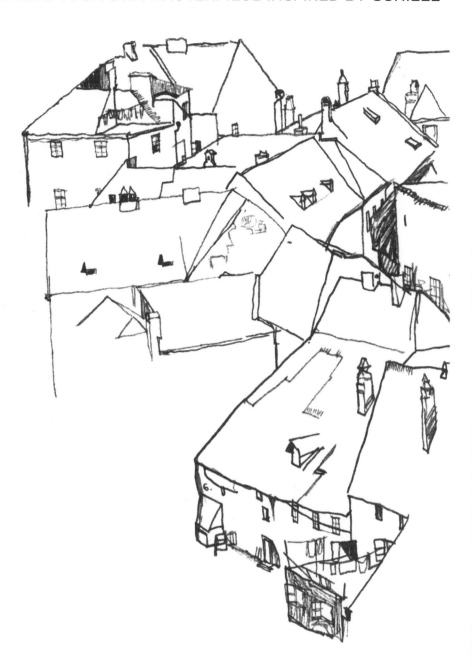

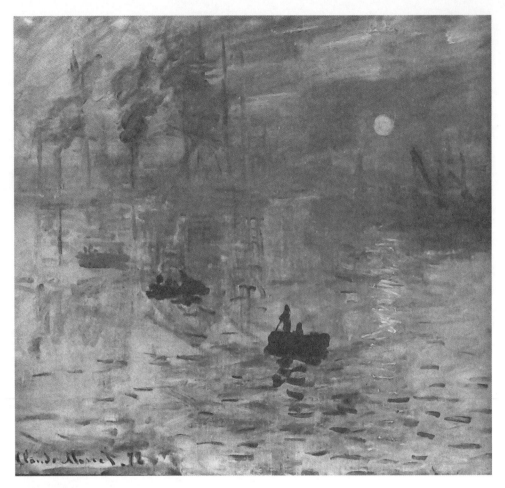

Rising Sun, 1872

Monet

(1840–1926)

Claude Monet, a French Impressionist painter, developed a love for painting *en pleine air*, or outdoors, in natural light. Inspired by landscape artists including Turner and Constable, he developed a loose and vivid style, capturing moments from nature. It was Monet's own work, *Impression: Sunrise*, that gave its name to the Impressionist movement. He often painted the same landscape repeatedly, each version showing a different quality of light, shadow, and atmosphere. His subject matter was as much the light on his subjects as the subjects themselves, and his paintings use a wide variety of colors to convey this; for instance, green leaves on a tree might be depicted in purple or yellow. To create shadow, rather than add black, Monet mixed complementary colors: yellow with purple, orange with blue, or red with green. Mixing colors quickly and painting using short, loose strokes, he was less concerned with creating a photographic reality than capturing an impression of what he saw.

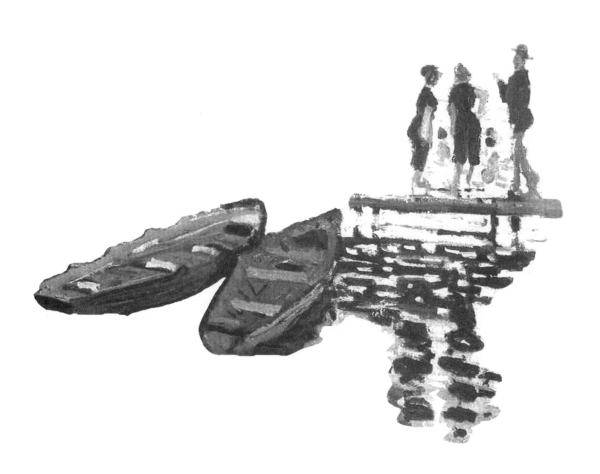

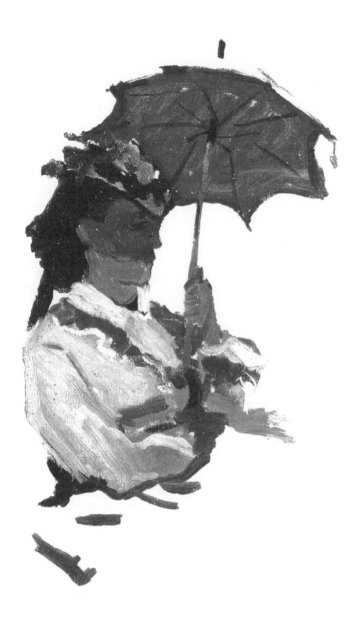

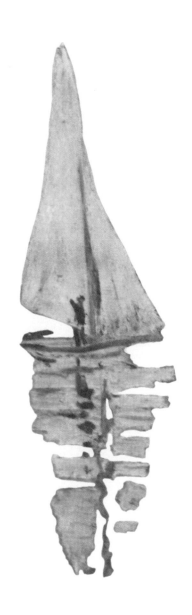

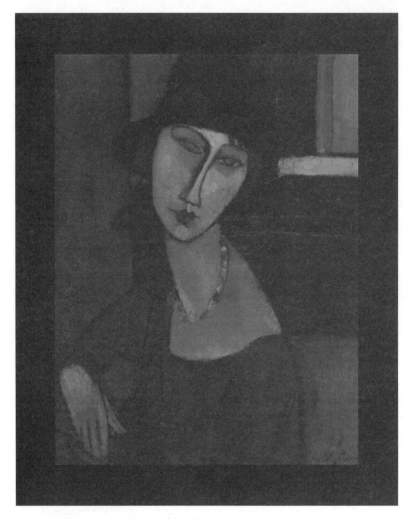

Jeanne Hébuterne with Hat and Necklace, 1917

Modigliani
(1884–1920)

Amedeo Modigliani was an Italian painter and sculptor. In his youth he studied the Italian Renaissance artists as well as the French Impressionists. He left Italy for Paris, and discovered the work of Cézanne and Picasso, who had an important effect on his style. For a while he focused on creating sculptures, carving faces in stone that closely resembled African masks. When his attention reverted back to painting, his sculpting style crept into his pictures. Modigliani's subjects were usually his friends or people from the local area. He would paint them with long faces and almond-shaped eyes, and usually gave his figures elongated necks and limbs. Modigliani's color palette was bold and, rather than using shading to give depth to his paintings, he would cleverly place strong colors side by side to create an illusion of perspective. Some colors would leap out of the canvas, while others appeared more distant.

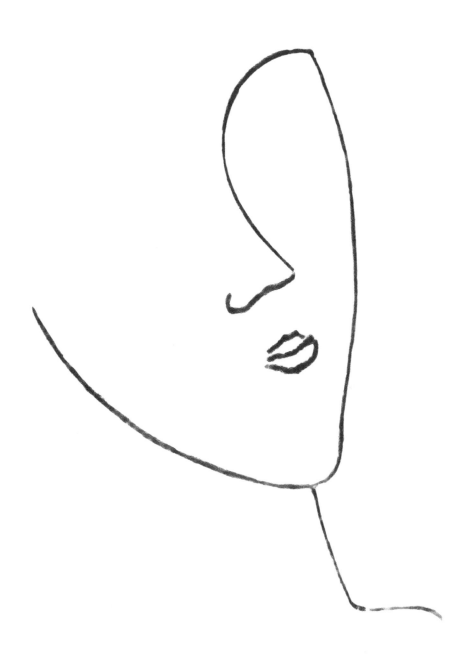

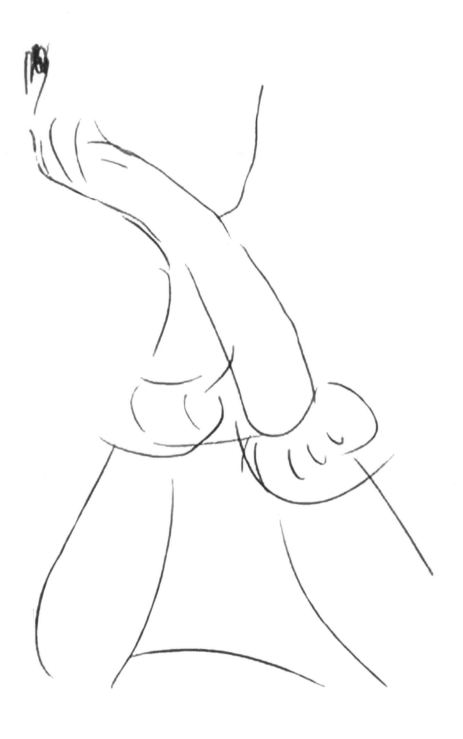

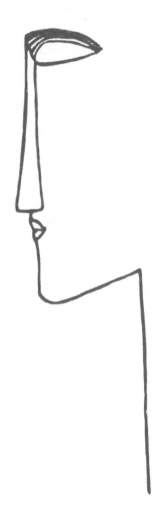

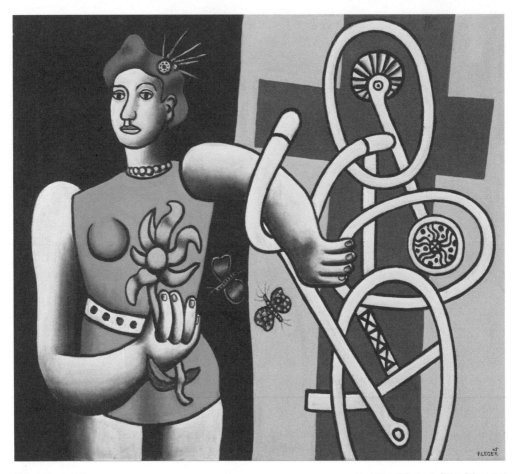

Big Julie, 1945

Léger
(1881–1955)

Fernand Léger was a French artist working in Paris. As well as painting on canvas, he designed theater sets and stained glass, painted murals, and even tried film-making. Léger believed in making art for the working class rather than just for rich people and collectors. When he began painting, he tried to use the popular style of the Impressionists, but Cézanne's exhibition in 1907 inspired him to change his methods. After learning about Picasso and Braque, the founders of Cubism, he began to paint more like them, building his pictures around tube shapes, which led some people to mock his style as "Tubism." After serving in the French army during the first World War, he began using even more unusual shapes. Rather than painting what he saw, Léger made symbolic paintings of modern city life using thick, dark outlines and solid colors. Fascinated by mechanical objects such as guns, engines, wheels, and gears, he liked to depict up-to-date subjects in surprising combinations.

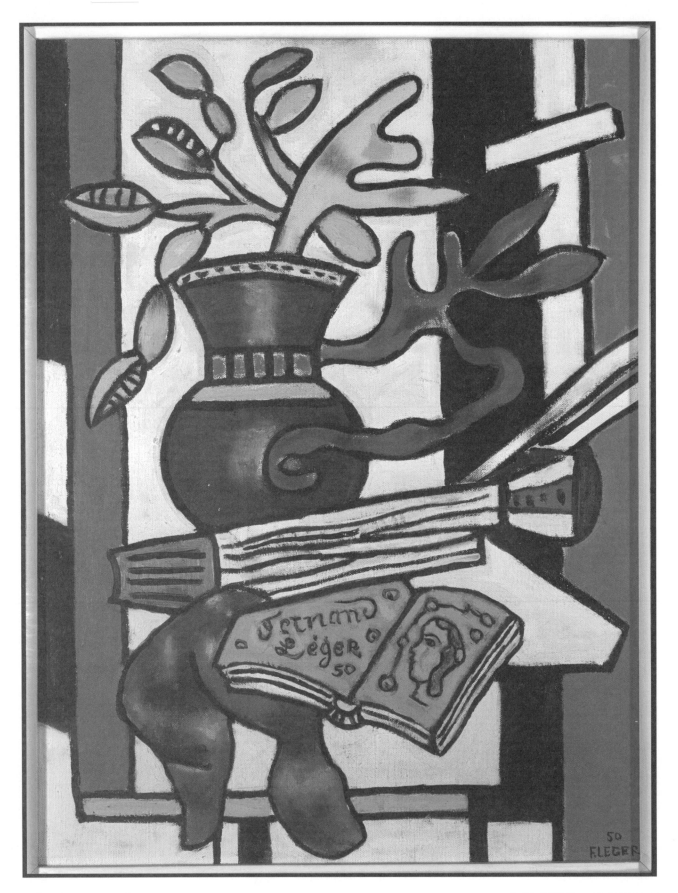

Yellow Flowers in a Blue Vase, 1950

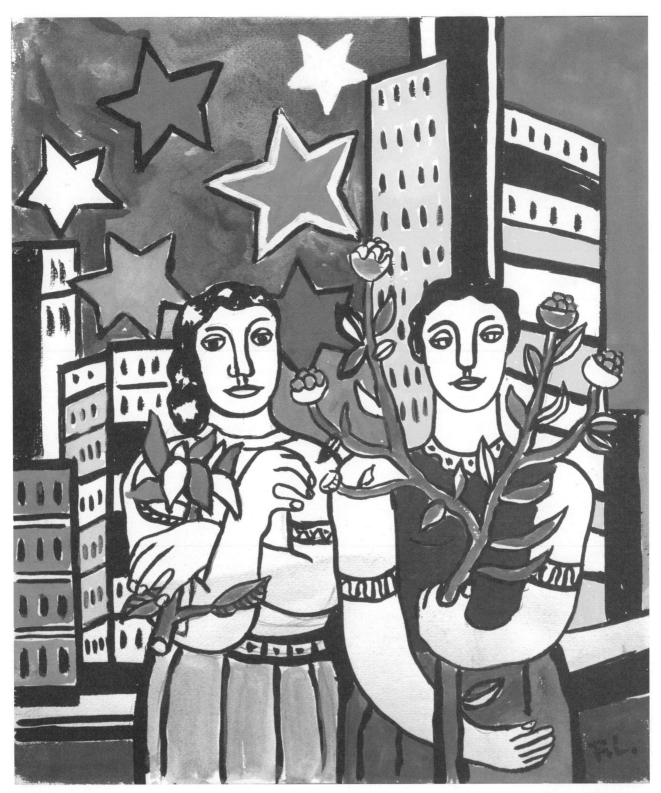

Two Figures with Flowers, date unknown

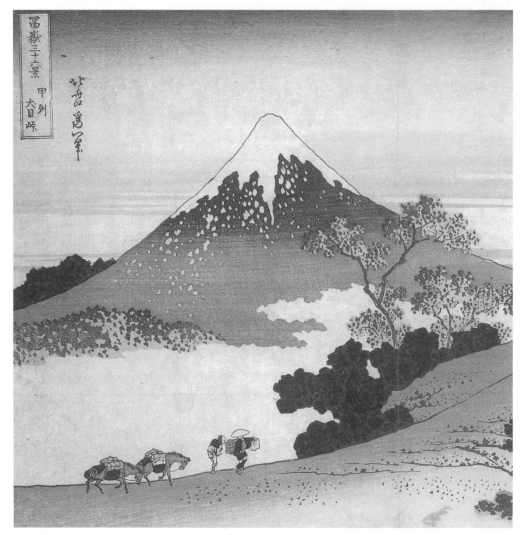

Inume Pass in Kai Province, c.1831–34

Hokusai

(1760–1849)

Katsushika Hokusai began sketching at a young age and was later apprenticed to Katsukawa Shunsho, a renowned artist in Japan in the late eighteenth century. He learned the traditional Japanese arts, including brush-painting techniques and woodblock printing. A craftsman as well as an artist, his work is that of a perfectionist, involving immense planning and detail to produce artwork in a style known as *ukiyo-e*, which translates as "pictures of the floating world." Interested in the work of European painters, particularly the Impressionists, he broke from artistic Japanese traditions and developed his own modern, individual style, making multiple prints and paintings of popular places and everyday life. His work *Thirty-six Views of Mount Fuji* was enormously popular and secured his fame and influence.

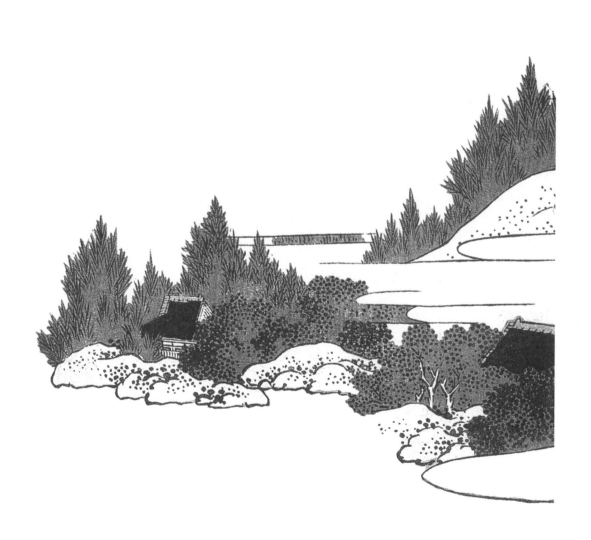

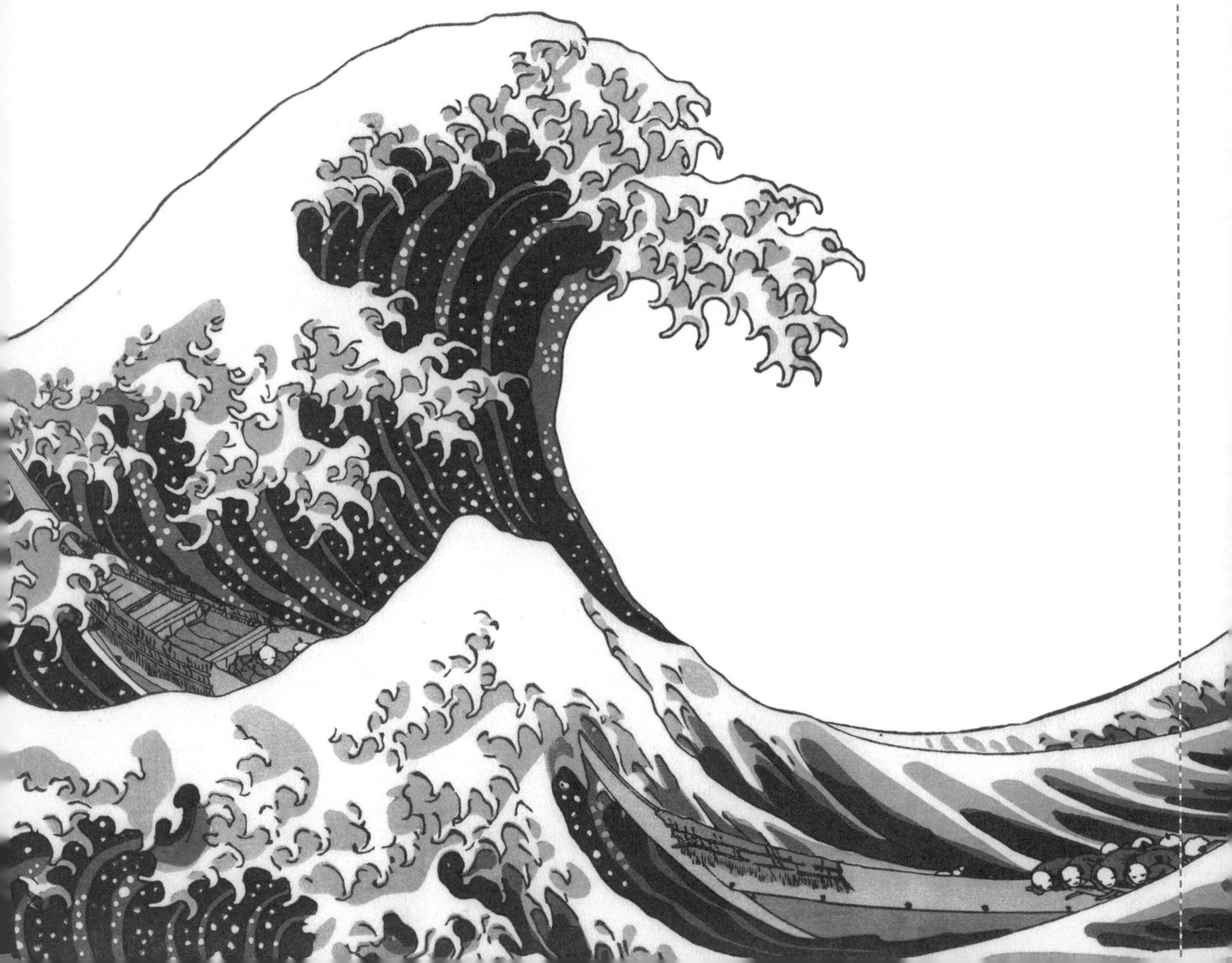

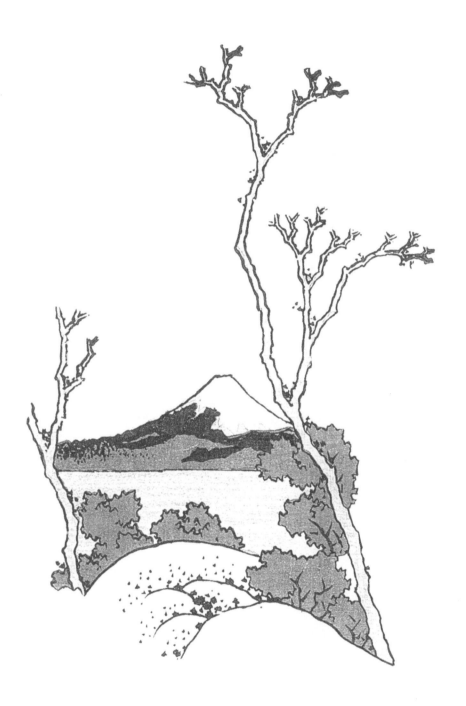

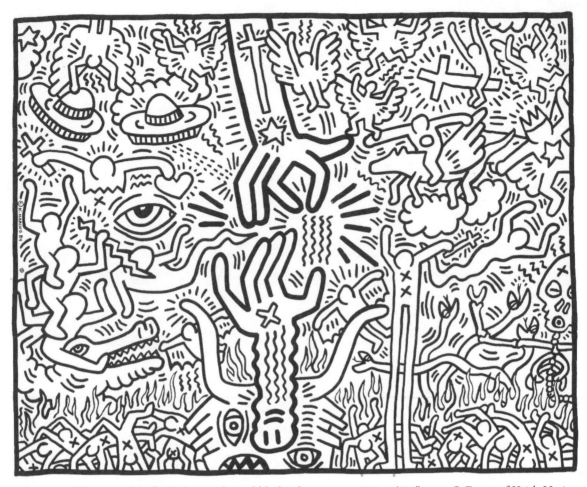

Marriage of Heaven and Hell, 1984, gouache and black ink on paper, 21¼ x 40¼"   © Estate of Keith Haring

Haring
(1958–1990)

The American artist Keith Haring became popular in the 1980s. In New York, graffiti artists were active throughout the city, and an alternative art scene sprang up around them. Haring was excited by the freedom of street art, and his pictures were full of figures painted in a cartoonlike style. Instead of painting on canvas and showing his work in art galleries, he took his lead from the graffiti artists, painting murals directly onto walls for the public to view. He even used chalk to draw on unused advertising boards on the subway, so that people could see art being created right in front of them, and he opened his own shop to sell his work to the public. Wherever he painted, Haring would cover a space with bold and complicated black lines, together with signs and symbols representing the busy city life around him. He showed his work in many unusual settings, from New York's nightclubs to music videos, and even produced a mural for the Berlin Wall.

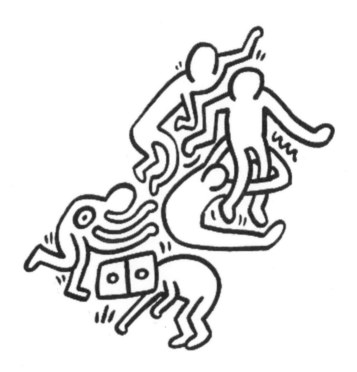

Untitled, 1990, sumi ink on board, 38½ x 60" [detail] © Estate of Keith Haring

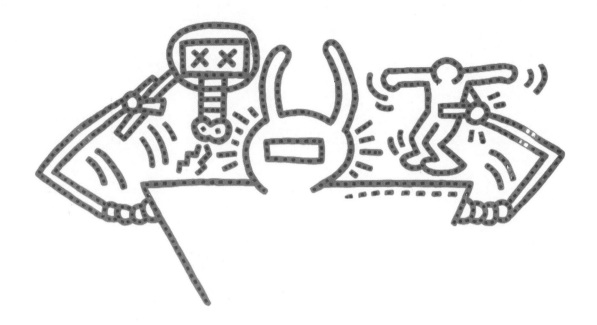

Untitled, 1983, vinyl ink on vinyl tarpaulin, 84 x 84" [detail] © Estate of Keith Haring

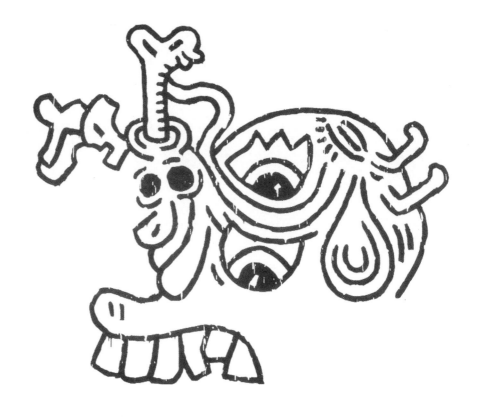

Untitled, 1984, acrylic on canvas, 120 x 120" [detail] © Estate of Keith Haring

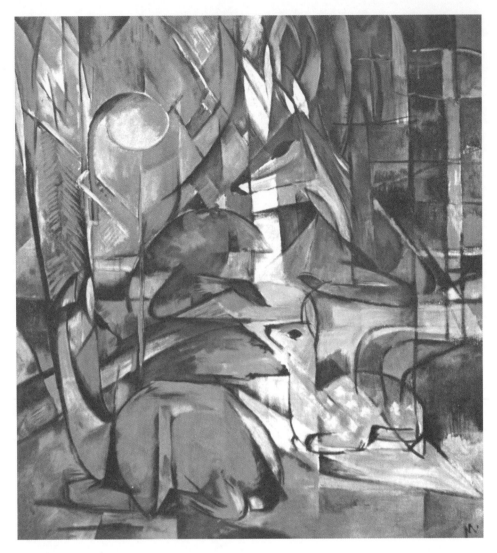

Deer in the Forest II, 1914

Marc
(1880–1916)

German artist Franz Marc was particularly influenced by the Cubist and Expressionist movements of the twentieth century and was keen to experiment with their theories of abstraction. A great friend of Kandinsky and a founder member of the Blue Rider group, Marc usually painted animals in natural settings, using mainly red, blue, and yellow, with each primary color having its own symbolic meaning. He liked to paint his subject from many angles, appearing to break it into pieces and depicting a different viewpoint in each section. Marc was also interested in "primitive" art, especially the paintings of untrained artists such as children or those suffering from psychiatric disorders. It was from these sources that he took his inspiration and he tried to fill his work with the same fantastical and emotional qualities.

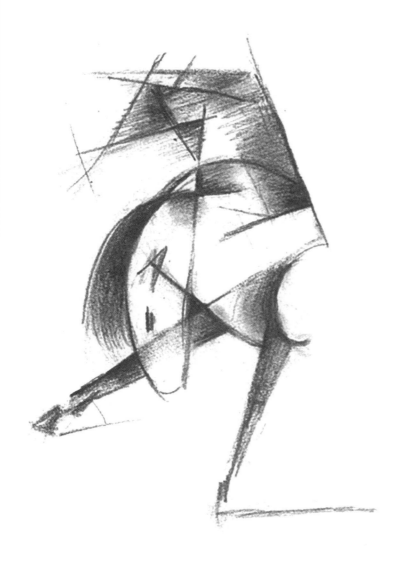

MARC

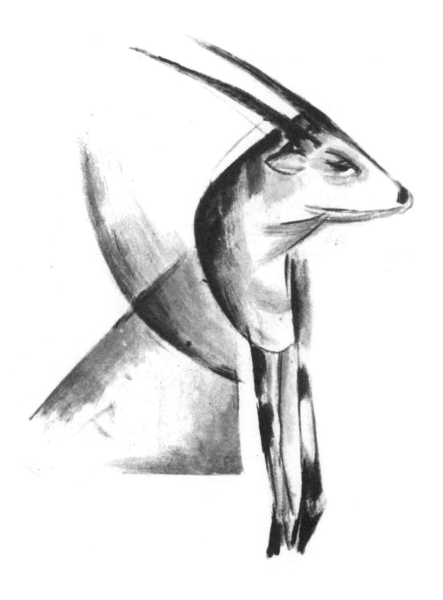

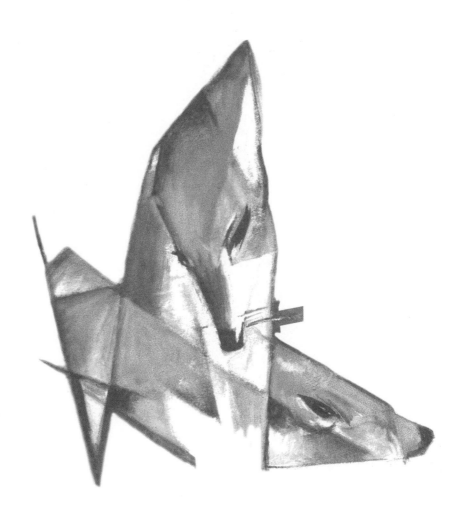

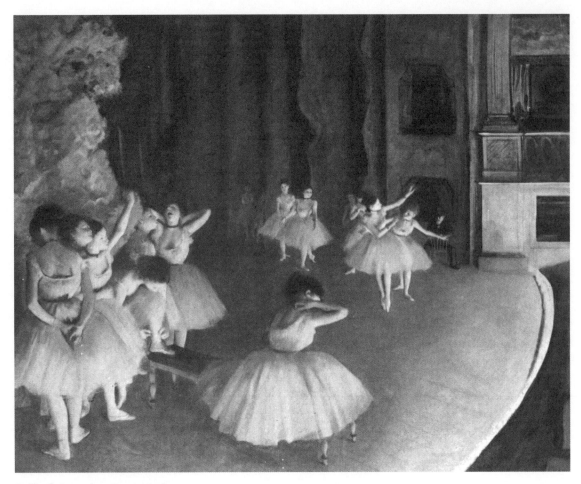

Ballet Rehearsal on Stage, 1874

Degas
(1834–1917)

Hilaire-Germain-Edgar De Gas, commonly known as Edgar Degas, was a member of the French Impressionist movement, though he did not share their popular passion for working outdoors. He rarely painted landscapes, nor the traditional formal portraits of the academic painters of his time. He opted for a less traditional subject matter, capturing the Parisian world around him. Combining his excellent understanding of the human figure with observations of modern-day settings, he depicted the Parisian nightlife, cafés, the ballet, horse races, and workers such as laundry women, bar staff, and shop owners. Degas would often make sketches and refer to them while painting in his studio. In his work he experimented with many materials: for instance, working with pastels on cardboard, sometimes adding paint to a charcoal drawing, or layering glazes of color one on top of the other.

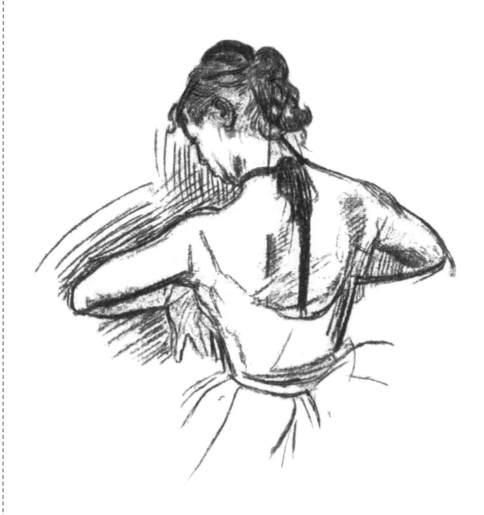

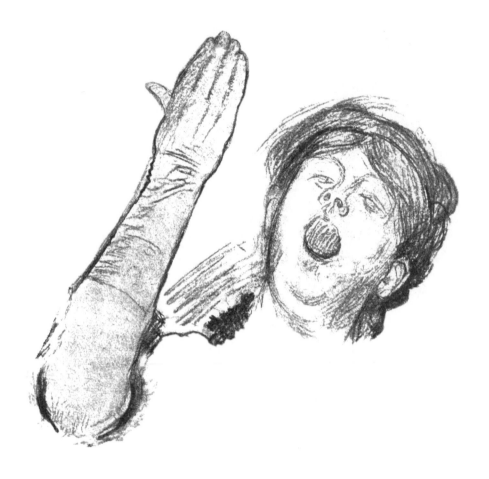

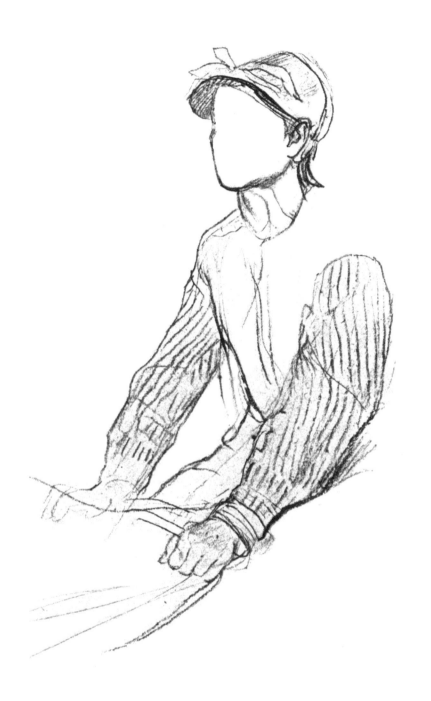

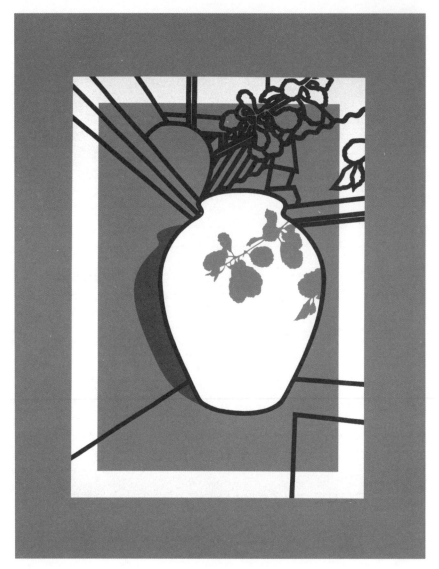

White Pot, 1976   © The Estate of Patrick Caulfield/DACS 2007

Caulfield
(1936–2005)

Both a painter and printmaker, Patrick Caulfield is widely regarded as having been a central figure in Britain's Pop Art movement of the 1960s. Using ordinary, traditional subjects, such as a vase or a bowl of fruit, he depicted them with smooth, clear outlines rather than in photographic detail. In addition, he painted technically brilliant interiors, demonstrating an interest in design and architecture. Because his drawing style is extremely precise and his pictures are composed with such care and thought, they can appear deceptively simple. Caulfield's paintings are large in scale, and he would often use just one or two colors over the whole work, striving to ensure that it was almost impossible to detect the brushstrokes.

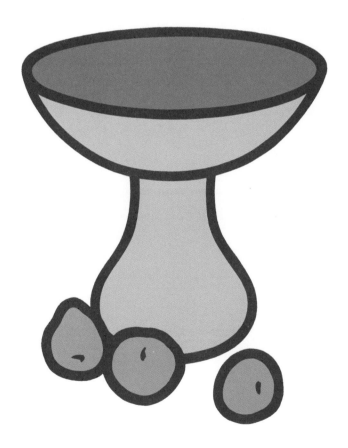

Fruit and Bowl, 1979–80 [detail] © The Estate of Patrick Caulfield/DACS 2007

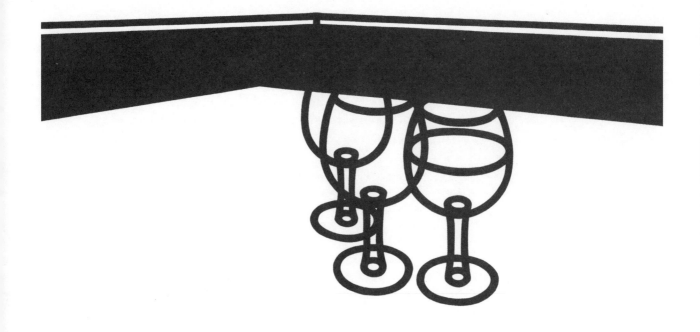

Black and White Café, 1973 [detail] © The Estate of Patrick Caulfield/DACS 2007

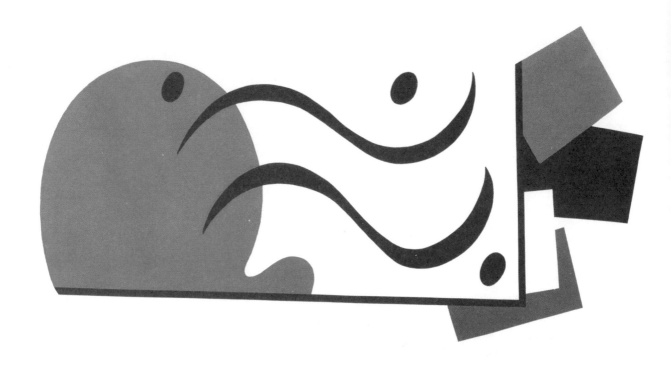

Artist's Studio, 1964 [detail] © The Estate of Patrick Caulfield/DACS 2007

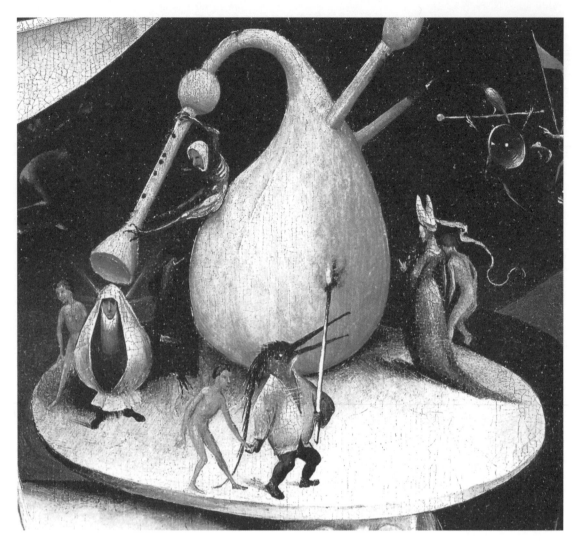

The Garden of Earthly Delights, c.1480–90 [detail]

Bosch

(1450–1516)

Hieronymus Bosch was the name adopted by Jerome van Aken, a Dutch painter who was prolific in the late Middle Ages. He was a devout and highly moral Catholic who was known for his unique artistic style, which involved creating startling, symbolic images of important religious scenes. His paintings often showed people battling with temptation and struggling against sin. The characters include demons, magicians, and peculiar, imaginative creatures crafted from strange combinations of animals, humans, birds, and vegetables, all set within detailed fantastical scenes of paradise and hell. The dreamlike images he produced were so surreal that some people believed he must have been involved with a religious cult. However, in reality, his visual storytelling and artistic imagination were simply far ahead of his time.

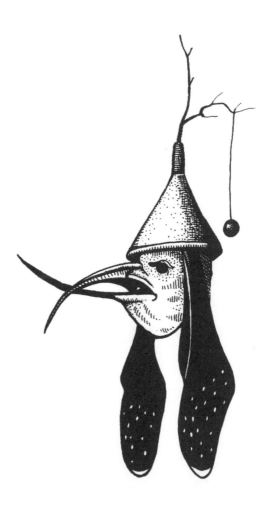

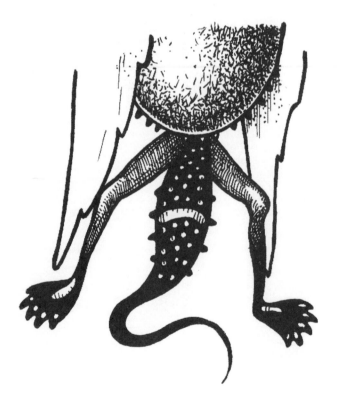

BOSCH

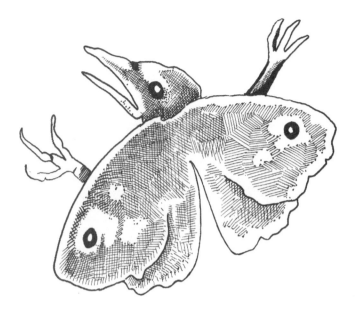

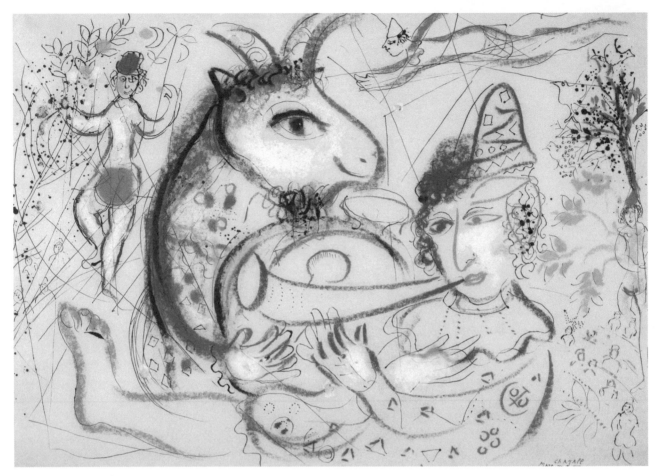

Circus, 1960

Chagall
(1887–1985)

Marc Chagall was a painter and printmaker from Belarus, near Poland, although most of his working life was spent in France. Surrounded by brilliant avant-garde artists he felt free to experiment and, rather than painting from real life, he made imaginative montages of his own ideas and dreams. As a painter he had a very creative style, alternating between delicate pinpoints of paint and bold, sweeping strokes of the brush. He created different textures by using wet splatters of paint or by scrubbing dry brushes across the canvas. He filled his pictures with unusual objects, animals, and people from his memories and from folk tales. He also used many symbols, creating his own painted language. In Chagall's works, trees represent life, the circus creativity, and horses freedom. Besides painting, Chagall also made a living from printmaking and illustrating, as well as designing stained glass and theater sets.

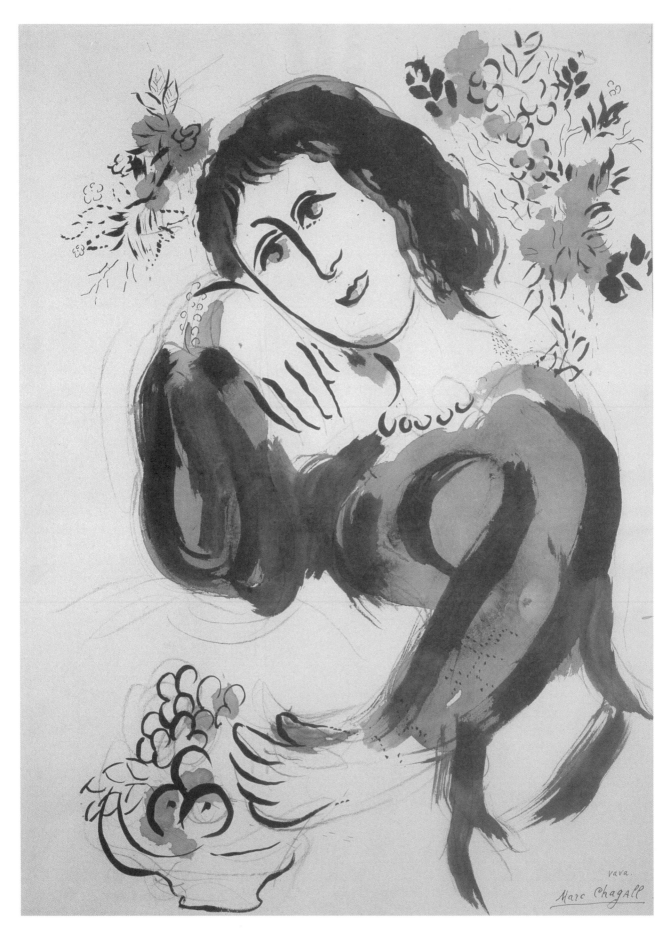

Vava, 1964

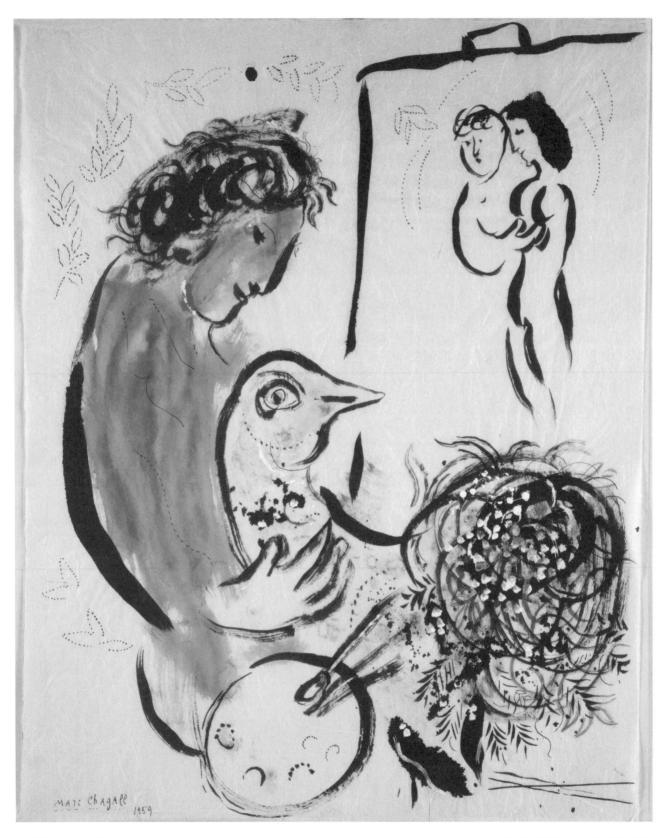

Self-Portrait, 1959

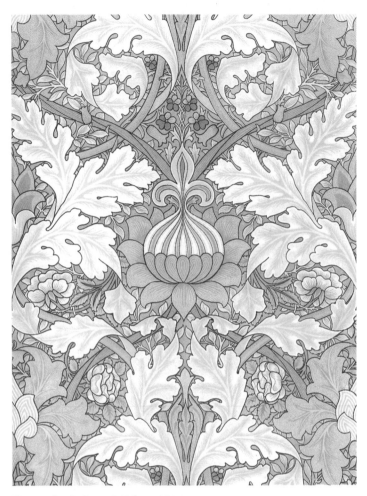

Design for St. James's Palace, 1881

Morris

(1834–96)

British artist and designer William Morris began his career at an architecture firm, where he gained a solid understanding of interior design. After leaving the company, he set up an artists' association with some friends and took orders from all over Britain for anything from stained glass and embroideries to furniture designs. This marked the start of the Arts and Crafts Movement, a social and artistic group that believed in traditional handcrafted products for the home, which was directly opposed to the Victorian trend for industrial manufacturing. In order to develop more unusual color combinations for printing, Morris experimented with paper-dyeing techniques. His designs were extremely complicated and involved intricate patterns, cleverly interlocking and repeating. They were based on scenes from nature, particularly leaves, flowers, and birds, and drawn in an ornate and decorative style. Today Morris is still best known for his unique wallpaper and textile designs.

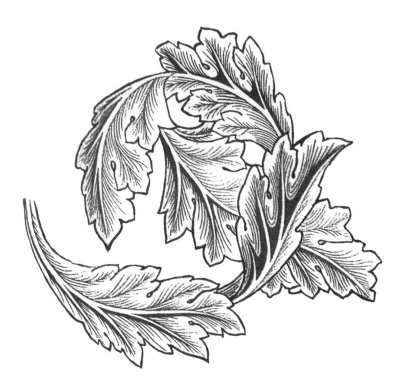

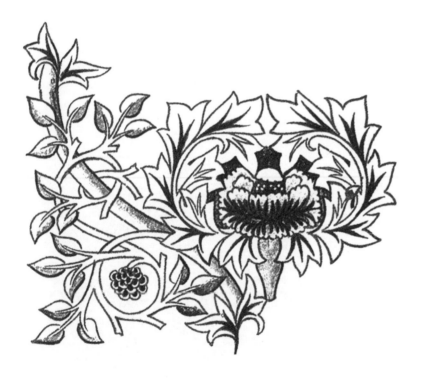

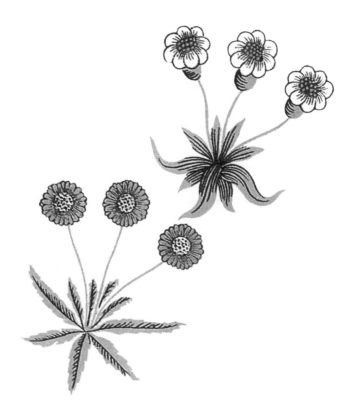

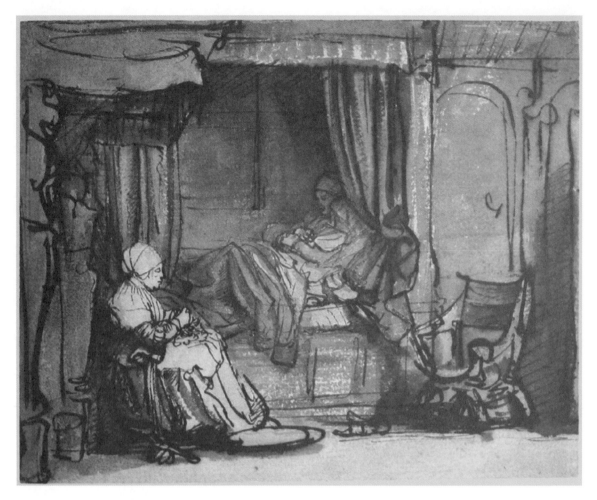

An Interior with a Woman in Bed, c.1640–41

Rembrandt
(1606–69)

Rembrandt van Rijn was a portrait painter and print-maker who lived and worked in the Netherlands. Interested in Italian art, he was inspired by the work of Leonardo da Vinci, particularly the way da Vinci composed his scenes. Rembrandt's compositions, in turn, were to become admired by future artists. He was a master of chiaroscuro, the arrangement of light and shade, and used this technique to highlight the important elements or figures in his pictures. Among his common subjects were traditional scenes from the Bible, history, and classical literature, and there are numerous paintings and etchings of people whom he came across in everyday life, as well as his own self-portraits. Rembrandt's great skill was in being able to depict ordinary people, full of character, in their natural environment.

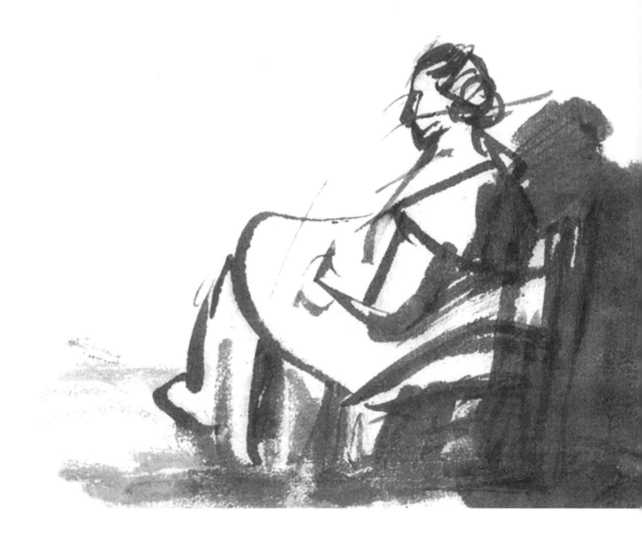

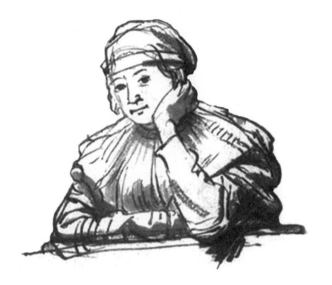

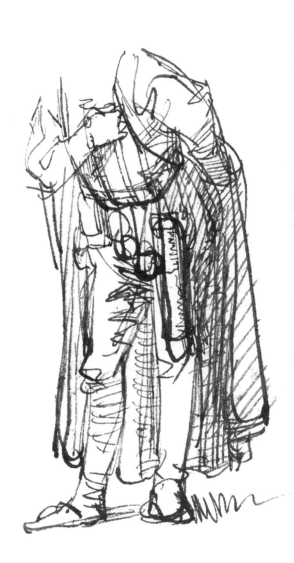

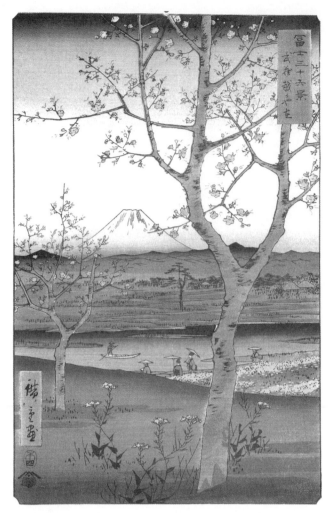

In the Countryside of Koshigaya, Thirty-six Views of Mount Fuji, c.1858–59

Hiroshige

(1797–1858)

Ando (or Utagawa) Hiroshige worked in the *ukiyo-e* style, documenting everyday life in Japan. He used traditional woodblock printing methods, building up prints using layers of different colors until the completed image was formed. To create textures and shading, Hiroshige used techniques such as adding glue to the ink, which gave transparency to a layer of color and revealed the layer below. This allowed him to add depth to his images. He reduced scenes to ornamental groupings of simplified lines and shapes, which were considered calming to look at. At a time when Japan was becoming more open to Western influences, Hiroshige was able to discover European painting techniques. The Impressionist artists particularly interested him, and he incorporated elements of their styles into his work, including single-point perspective, which previously had rarely been used in Japanese art.

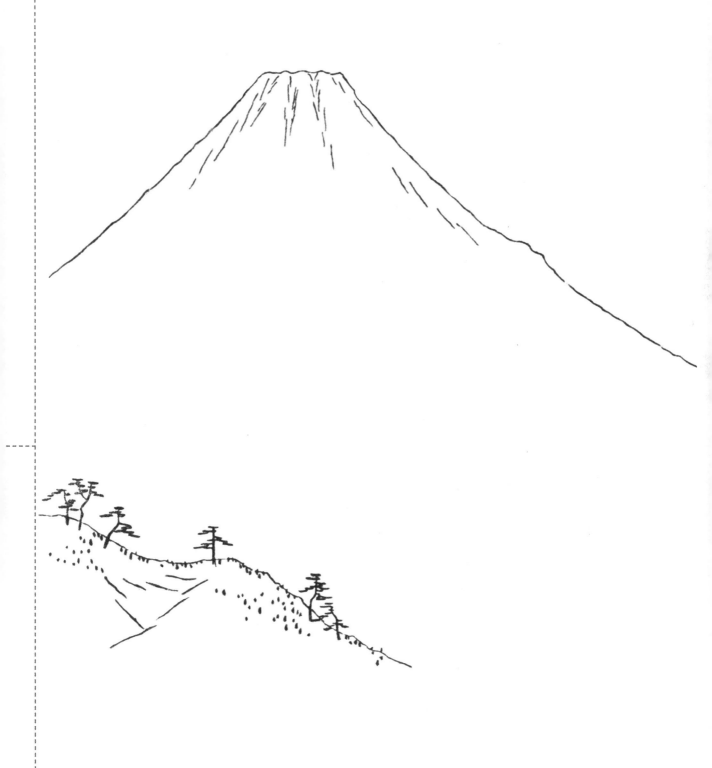

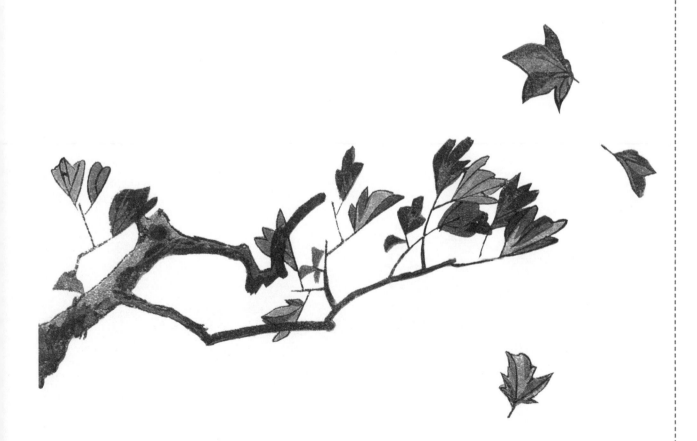

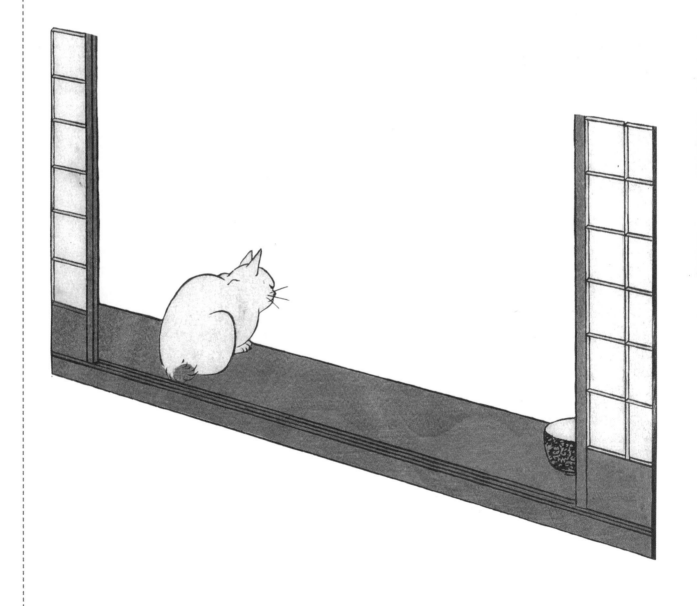

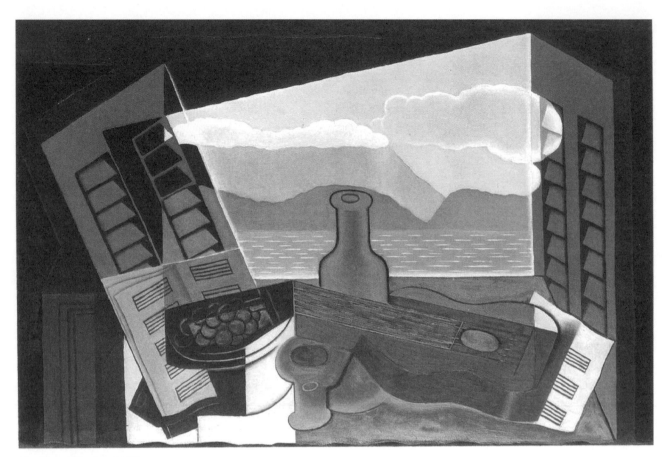

The Open Window, 1921

Gris
(1887–1927)

José Victoriano González-Pérez was a Spanish Cubist artist. He became interested in art when he was a teenager and moved to Paris to paint. He worked for most of his life in France under the name Juan Gris. When he worked, Gris chose objects that he wanted to paint and arranged them in a purposeful grouping, a "still life." He carefully drew a frame of rectangles, squares, triangles, and other geometric shapes onto his canvas and painted different views of his still life into each shape. Gris employed similar Cubist techniques to those of Picasso, but he preferred to use much richer colors in his paintings. Always trying to further his style, when collage became an important part of Picasso's paintings, Gris similarly and sometimes literally adopted this effect into his own work. For instance, if his still life contained a mirror, Gris might include a real piece of mirror in his painting. Although not a founder of Cubism, Gris took the style further, making it more popular.

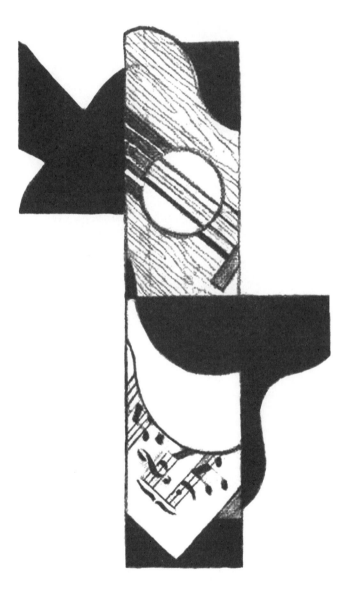

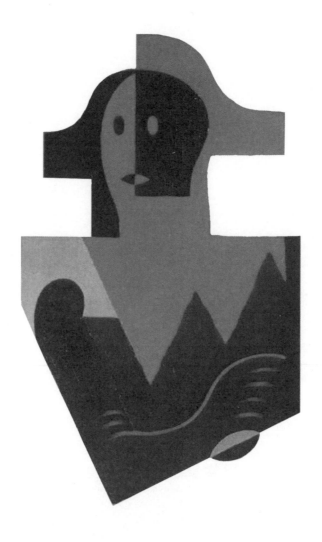

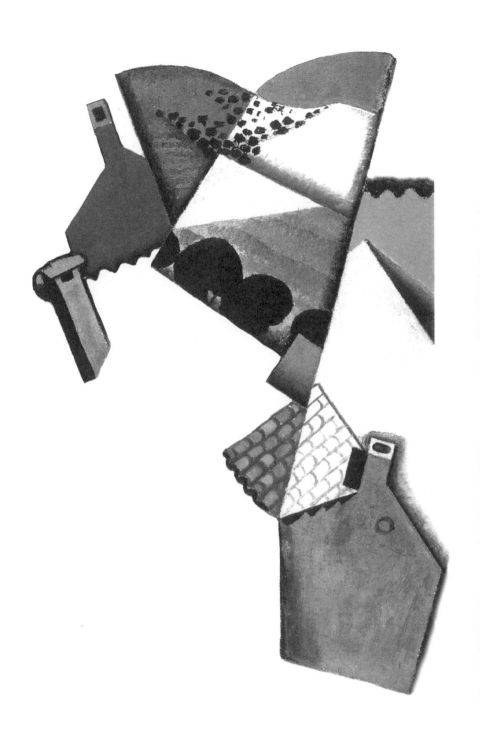

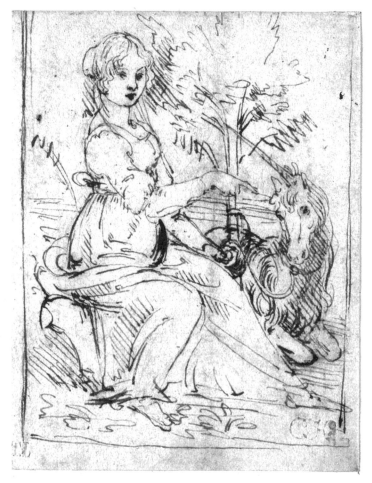

A Maiden with a Unicorn, late 1470s

da Vinci

(1452–1519)

Leonardo da Vinci, an extraordinarily talented child, was enrolled as an apprentice to an artist's studio while still only in his late teens. There he learned the many skills of a craftsman—from metalworking to carpentry, as well as painting, drawing, and sculpting. Leonardo spent hours practicing his drawing skills and kept a sketchbook in which he would draft anything interesting that he observed. His fascination with the human form led him to study anatomy, and he would even dissect corpses to gain a better understanding of the body. This scientific approach to painting and drawing meant that Leonardo's figures looked more natural than those sketched by his contemporaries, which reflected his greater knowledge of the structure and composition of the human form. Furthermore, Leonardo's technical abilities allowed him to achieve more emotional facial expressions, natural personality, and accurate detail in his pictures.

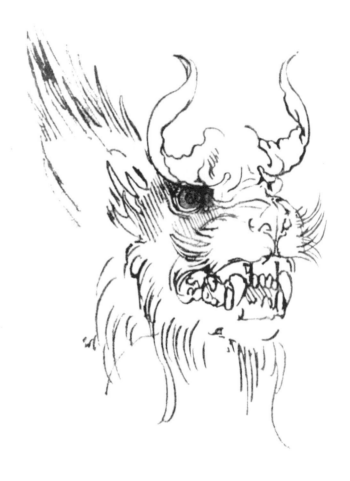

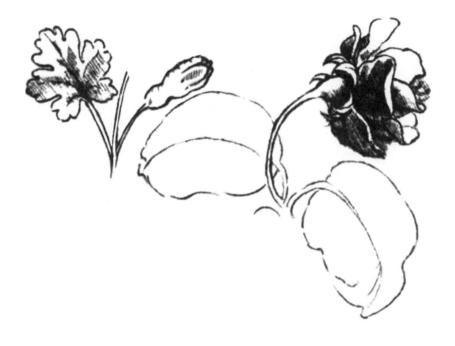

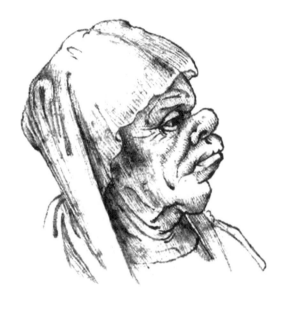
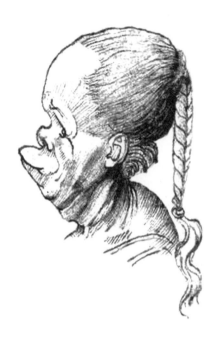

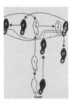
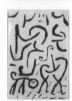

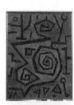
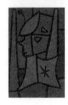

Paul Cézanne

The Sea at L'Estaque, 1886–90
Private collection

From *Gardanne*, 1885–86
Metropolitan Museum of Art, New York

From *Man with a Pipe*, c.1892–95
Private Collection

From *Still Life*, c.1892–94
Tate Gallery, London

Vincent van Gogh

Road with Cypress and Star, 1890
Rijksmuseum Kröller-Müller, OtterloFrom *Cypresses, Saint-Rémy*, 1889
Brooklyn Museum, New York

From *Boats at Sea, Saintes-Maries-de-la-Mer*, 1888
Musées Royaux des Beaux-Arts de Belgique, Brussels

From *The Starry Night*, 1889
The Museum of Modern Art, New York

From *The Road to Tarascon*, 1888
Solomon R. Guggenheim Museum, New York

From *Café Terrace on the Place du Forum*, 1888
Dallas Museum of Art

Joan Miró

Woman Dreaming of Escape, 1945
Photo © Archivo Iconografico, S.A./Corbis

Composition with the Moon Blue, 1949
Photo © Christie's Images/Corbis

Large Figure and Blue Moon, date unknown
Photo © Burstein Collection/Corbis

Egon Schiele

Portrait of the Artist's Wife, Seated, 1918
Österreichische Galerie, Vienna

From *Adele Harms in a Striped Dress, Seated*, 1917

From *Drawing a Nude Model Before a Mirror*, 1910

From a sketch for *Krumau Town Crescent I*, 1914

Claude Monet

Rising Sun, 1872
Musée Marmottan, Paris

From *Bathers at Le Grenouillère*, 1869
National Gallery, London

From *The Beach at Trouville*, 1870
National Gallery, London

From *Regatta at Argenteuil*, 1872
Musée d'Orsay, Paris

Amadeo Modigliani

Jeanne Hébuterne with Hat and Necklace, 1917
Private Collection

From *Head* (pen & ink on paper)
Private Collection

From *Woman, Head in Hand*, c.1917
Museum of Modern Art, New York

From *Female Head with Earring*
Private Collection

Fernand Léger

Big Julie, 1945
Photo © Museum of Modern Art, New York/Lauros/
Giraudon/The Bridgeman Art Library

Yellow Flowers in a Blue Vase, 1950
Photo © Private Collection/The Bridgeman Art Library

Two Figures with Flowers, date unknown
Photo © Private Collection/The Bridgeman Art Library

Katsushika Hokusai

Inume Pass in Kai Province,
from the series *Thirty-six Views of Mount Fuji*, c.1831–34
Public Collection

From *Hakone Lake in Sagami Province*,
from the series *Thirty-six Views of Mount Fuji*, c.1831–34
Public Collection

From *Cresting Wave off the Coast of Kanagawa (The Great Wave)*,
from the series *Thirty-six Views of Mount Fuji*, c.1831–34
Public Collection

From *Fuji from Gotenyama at Shinagawa on the Tokaido Road*,
from the series *Thirty-six Views of Mount Fuji*, c.1831–34
Public Collection

Keith Haring

All images by kind courtesy of the Estate of Keith Haring.

Franz Marc

Deer in the Forest II, 1914
Staatliche Kunsthalle, Karlsruhe

From *Horse*, 1913
Sketchbook XXIX
University of Göttingen Art Collection

From *Resting Antelope*, 1912

From *Foxes*, 1913
Kunstmuseum, Düsseldorf

Edgar Degas

Ballet Rehearsal on Stage, 1874
Musée d'Orsay, Paris

From *Standing Dancer, Seen from Behind*, c.1872

From *Café-Concert Singer*, c.1878–80

From *Young Jockey*, c.1866–68